MW01257948

"*My lette servi* Cold war. This story, about a man born with 'boats in his heart' and resolute devoutness to his lifelong love, is one filled with optimism, inspiration, and is well worth reading."

— Scott McGaugh, *New York Times* bestselling author of *USS Midway: America's Shield*

"*My Dearest Bea* offers a window into a little-seen slice of life during the Cold and Korean Wars, between two people new to the service and the sacrifices military life entails, as well as new to marriage. Above all, the letters reveal a sailor who longed for his wife, a time-less tale to which every military family—then and now —can relate."

— Kate Lewis, Book Critic, *Military Families Magazine*

"Peyton Roberts allows us special access into the romance between her grandparents with her edited collection of letters in *My Dearest Bea*. In them, mili-tary-affiliated people will see themselves, as I did, for these letters captured the essence of service, duty, longing, and love. *My Dearest Bea* is a treasure!"

— Tif Marcelo, *USA Today* bestselling author of *In a Book Club Far Away*

"All the best love stories start with a sailor, because loving a sailor means that you often love for months with words alone. The love story is universal, made more intense by the kind of longing young military couples have felt through the ages. This is a tale that will bring back your own love story in vivid color."

— Jacey Eckhart, author of *The Homefront Club*

"This book is a beautiful collection of love letters written from a Navy musician to his wife in the 1950's. But it is more than that. It's a reflection on the way a loving relationship can impact family members for several generations. It's a commentary on the ways military life has changed, yet the emotional struggles remain the same. *My Dearest Bea* is a testimony to the lasting value of handwritten letters."

— Lizann Lightfoot, author of *Open When: Letters of Encouragement for Military Spouses*

"A beautifully annotated collection of love letters from the editor's beloved grandfather to his wife, penned while he served as a musician in the Navy during the Korean War. As a Navy spouse herself, Peyton has brought to this project an understanding of the many sacrifices service families make. This special bond with her grandparents and their influence on her life unfold through the deeply personal prose she has woven throughout the letters."

— Lisa Franco, author of *My Dearest Darling: Letters of Love in Wartime*

"Through Bill Holston's letters and Roberts's reflections in *My Dearest Bea*, today's military couples will find encouragement for a season apart. Better still is a rare opportunity to relive what prompted the separation in the first place—their own love story."

— Kathryn Butler, Book Review, We Are the Mighty

"Navy wife Peyton Roberts writes in her book *My Dearest Bea* that the hardship of military life sometimes bears unexpected gifts. Peyton has taken one of those gifts—a trove of love letters from her grandfather as a young sailor at sea to his beloved wife at home—and has turned it into another. Weaving her own reflections and her grandfather's letters into a poignant expression of love and loss, the author has created an homage to the grandparents who made her childhood 'magical.'"

— Terri Barnes, author of *Spouse Calls: Messages From a Military Life*

Love Letters from the
USS Midway 1951–1952

My Dearest Bea

Edited by
PEYTON H. ROBERTS

Foreword by
KARL ZINGHEIM,
USS Midway Museum

My Dearest Bea

Love Letters from the USS *Midway*
1951 – 1952

Edited by Peyton H. Roberts
Foreword by Karl Zingheim

ANCHOR LINE
PRESS

My Dearest Bea

© 2024 by Peyton H. Roberts

Published in Virginia Beach, Virginia, by Anchor Line Press, LLC

Library of Congress Control Number: 2024902099

Paperback ISBN 978-1-963595-00-0

Hardcover ISBN 978-1-963595-02-4

eBook ISBN 978-1-963595-01-7

Printed in the United States of America.

Book cover design by Melissa Williams Designs

Cover photography by Adam Winkel

Artistic direction by Courtney Holston-Toth

To the children in our lives—

May you find in these pages
a glimpse of the great-grandparents
who would have loved and adored you
above all else.

U. S. S. MIDWAY

Acknowledgments

I owe a heap of thanks to several amazing people who helped this story come together. For starters, I am endlessly grateful to my sister, Courtney, for finding and safeguarding these letters. They (and you) will forever be one of the greatest treasures of my life.

Over the years, my mother, Jane Holston, read and edited several rounds of this collection and provided invaluable insight. It has been a tremendous joy to work on another heart project with my all-time favorite author.

My husband, Nick, helped explain military terms and nuances of Navy life. I am so thankful for his all-in support of my writing. And for this wild journey of Navy service we've endured together, for worse and for better.

The USS *Midway's* historian Karl Zingheim answered questions that my research couldn't. The foreword he wrote shares deeper insight about the *Midway* and the Navy Band during this time in history. I am beyond grateful for his contributions. Additional help with research and photographs came from the archivist at Virginia Beach Public Library.

Turning a story into a book is no small feat. Thanks to Linda Fulkerson, my publisher from Scrivenings Press, for lending her expertise to help this story cross the finish line.

Having the cover designed by artist Melissa Williams and featured in *Publisher's Weekly* was a tremendous surprise. Her gorgeous design feels like the perfect tribute to my grandparents' love for one another, and I adore what she created.

Extra thanks to Adam Winkel for photographing and

preserving these priceless letters and family photos into archive quality images that were used on the cover. The fact that the cover was posted to *Publisher's Weekly* on April 7 —Bea and Shoopa's anniversary—seemed to affirm that their letters wished to be read.

I am so thankful for the support and encouragement of my aunt, Wendy Holston, and my cousins, Chris and Erika, and other contributing family members to make this collection of letters available to readers. We hope these letters are enjoyed by our grandparents' students and friends as well as service members and their families, letter lovers, and history enthusiasts.

My grandparents devoted their lives to faith, family, and education. It is in this spirit of love and learning that we send Bea and Shoopa's words out into the world to be read, contemplated, and cherished.

"I'm sure going to miss you. I don't know how I ever enjoyed life before I met you."

William J. Holston, USS Midway, October 1951

Foreword

Between these pages is a love story preserved in the transcribed letters of a young man serving a hitch in the Navy during the Korean War era. William "Shoopa" Holston grew up in Depression-era Lynchburg, Virginia, a town nestled in the Blue Ridge foothills on a bank of the James River. As Peyton Roberts, his granddaughter, notes, this idyllic setting inspired an intelligent and unconventional boy to embark on a lifetime affinity for boats. A penchant for musical performance offered young Bill a ticket to a momentary fusing of his two interests with service in the Navy as a musician. While training at Washington, D.C., Bill met his future wife, Beatrice McGlasson.

After training, Bill reported for sea duty as part of the U.S.S. *Midway*'s band. In those years, capital ships like the *Midway* sported musical bands to perform for ceremonies, foreign port visits, and entertainment. Accomplished instrument performances were expected at all times, which meant that shipboard musicians were constantly practicing and rehearsing in between their appearances, which comes across in Bill's cursive, embossed beneath evocative "U.S.S. MIDWAY" letterhead.

Another aspect common among young sailors on their first enlistment is the impact of exposure to other cultures and exotic realms. Although Bill only served a single enlistment, this up-river country lad encountered extraordinary variety in the port calls the *Midway* made in the Caribbean and Mediterranean Seas. Another trait that shines forth is Bill's genuine passion for music—and his love for Bea. The fortuitous discovery of another letter from Bill to Bea, this time some fifteen years into their marriage, shows that their admiration and devotion to one another had not diminished in the slightest.

Peyton has not merely transcribed her grandfather's letters, she has researched the backstories of the situations described therein, and has provided a fine encapsulation of Bill and Bea's marriage and family memories of the couple. Time eventually took its toll on their health, with Bea passing on some four years before her beloved Bill in their old age, but Peyton prefers to reflect on her memories of this loving couple and their influence that lives on.

This compilation is also a testament to the written age, when physical messages between people can endure well beyond their intended purpose and continue to touch the lives of others ever after, a virtue the digital age may not emulate so admirably as in these letters to *My Dearest Bea.*

Karl Zingheim
USS Midway Museum

Preface

Sunday, December 21, 2002
Pensacola, Florida

The sun lowered toward the treetops on a blue-sky afternoon as my grandfather, whom I call Shoopa, limped to the end of the long wooden dock. In his hand was a single red rose. In his eye was a hint of mischief.

Beneath towering masts of two imposing sailboats, Shoopa steadied each footstep on the final stretch of dock. A smile snuck across his face as he tossed the rose into the salty, chocolate waters of Bayou Chico. The flower floated in place, unbothered by the current's gentle ripples.

A seagull called out overhead and a shrimping boat passed by in the distance as Shoopa returned to the house, his uneven gait slowing but never stopping him. Back over land, he lowered a cooler bag onto the grassy shore beside two overturned rowboats.

His preparations complete, he continued up the back steps to the house where he surprised my grandmother, Bea, with an invitation to join him on a boat ride.

I can just imagine Bea tidying up the beginnings of supper and grabbing a sweatshirt to come along. Given his track record of schemes, she would have certainly been suspecting her husband was up to something.

Shoopa's aging fleet consisted of everything from sailboats to houseboats, all of which were tied up to the dock or haphazardly stashed on shore. His boat collection even boasted a wooden Viking Ship—the only working replica of its kind in North America—decorated with authentic Nordic woodcarvings, which he made during summers off from teaching.

All decked out in oil-splattered pants and a signature paint shirt, Shoopa escorted his bride down the cinderblock steps to the shore. They stepped onto the small beach and into the vessel chosen for this outing, a shiny new dinghy, remarkably devoid of rust and seagull droppings and dried-up paint.

Before embarking on their voyage, Shoopa retrieved a bottle of champagne from the cooler and handed my grandmother a stem glass. Bea's eyes smiled beneath her golden curls as the Captain offered a too-grandiose-for-the-moment toast, quoting Keats or Shakespeare or Thoreau. For added fanfare, he may have even sung a few favorite lyrics of a long-forgotten show tune.

After helping Bea into the boat, Shoopa pushed off the sandy shore. Wooden oars in hand, he rowed past the Viking Ship, named the *Loki*—for the Norse god of mischief—and the massive steel-hulled sailboat, fittingly named the *Hulk*. Just beyond the dock, his clever surprise waited as planned.

Resting the oars, Shoopa leaned over the side of the rowboat and scooped up the long-stemmed red rose. He shook off a few salty drops of bayou water and handed the flower to Bea.

Bea blushed, accepting the rose with a hint of embarrassment. I imagine she was surprised ... but not completely surprised. The thoughtful gesture was on brand for this loyal but mischievous sailor she'd navigated the last 50-something years with.

During the tail end of their Sunday voyage, I stumbled upon their sweet date. I was visiting Pensacola for a few days on winter break from college and had just returned to my grandparents' house. Seeing their cars in the driveway but no one inside, I ventured out back where I spotted Shoopa rowing Bea back to shore.

In my purse that day, I happened to have a disposable camera. I snapped a quick photo of my grandparents in the dinghy to share with family.

Looking at that photo all these years later, I love that Bea is absolutely glowing here. And the sparkle in Shoopa's eyes reveals the overflow of love in his heart for his dearest companion.

Christmas on the Bayou, Shoopa titled the outing.

Over time, I would look back at this blue-sky afternoon on Bayou Chico, not just as a favorite memory of my grandparents, but also as one of many unforgettable scenes in a timeless love story.

Chapter 1

The First Letter

Location: The USS Midway off the Atlantic Coast of Florida, heading toward Cuba

Wednesday, May 23, 1951

My Dearest Darling,

> *The weather has gotten very hot and sticky. We must be nearing Florida.*

> *Last night we had some excitement. One of the Marines fell over the side and we all (the entire ship) had to go topside to muster. They finally found him swimming around. He was probably one scared Marine.*

> *We have been having a lot of drills. GQ's (General quarters) (battle stations that is), Fire drills, abandon ship and all types. We had a break and had to get up at only 6:00 this morning. The morning after I left you we had to get up at 4:30 A.M.!! We didn't get back to the ship until 1:00. I think we get to*

Cuba Saturday. I understand we go out in the daytime and come back in every night. I think I shall go fishing if possible.

Man I sure hated leaving you the other night. All I want is to get out of this ridiculous outfit. The only place I should be is at home with you. Let's face it, baby, I love you something terrible. You just make me flip, to put it mildly. I have never expected married life to begin to equal what I have experienced in the short time we've been married. We've really had a swell time, haven't we? I have so many pleasant memories that I shall always remember and treasure. And most of all, I have you, the sweetest lady a good gentleman ever had.

Say, honey, how's that new job coming? Tell me about it, huh?

They're about ready to turn the lights off so I'd better close for now. Be a sweet kid and I'll be home soon. I love you, my love, more than life itself.

All My Love,
Your Bill

Chapter 2

Introductions

Uncovering this treasure trove of love letters my grandfather wrote to my grandmother has been a greater gift than I could have ever imagined. For whole generations, no one else knew these letters existed.

An unexpected find brought them into my life at a serendipitous moment. By the time this collection was discovered and read, I was longing for bygone days on Bayou Chico and knee-deep in my own rollercoaster journey as a Navy spouse.

Each time I return to the heartfelt words on these pages, the unscripted display of Shoopa's never-ending love for Bea transports me to the warmth, music, and laughter that filled their home throughout my childhood. Year after year, new discoveries unfolded on each page, writing an epilogue in my heart of timeless lessons about life and love.

Before sharing the letters and reflections that follow, I would like to introduce my grandparents to those who are meeting them for the first time. Their individual stories began on separate continents, traversed the chaos of World War II, and brought them to this moment as a newly married

Navy couple beginning their adult lives together in Norfolk, Virginia.

There is nothing inherently extraordinary about their early journeys aside from the confluence of factors that brought them together and moored their hearts to each other for the rest of time.

My Dearest Bea

My grandmother, Beatrice McGlasson, had an unusual upbringing due to an unlikely meeting of her parents overseas. Bea's father, Clifford "Mac" McGlasson, was a U.S. vice consul who served at American embassies in Spain, Italy, Sweden, Switzerland, France, Czechoslovakia, and Egypt.

In 1926, when his younger brother died of tuberculosis at just 24 years old, Mac returned to his family home in Washington, D.C., to help his father with the burial. After a few months working at the State Department's headquarters, Mac was assigned to the U.S. Embassy in Prague.

There in the bustling 1920s social scene of post-WWI

Czechoslovakia, Mac fell deeply in love with an English-speaking Czech woman named Bozena (called Boija), the daughter of a prominent business owner in Prague's famous Old Towne Square. After a magical season of courtship, Boija accepted Mac's proposal, along with the instability and adventure of marriage and motherhood as a foreign diplomat's wife.

Mac and Boija's only child, Beatrice, was born in Lausanne, Switzerland, in 1930. Bea grew up living in Paris, traveling throughout Europe, and speaking three languages fluently.

Her storybook childhood ended in Bern, Switzerland, upon her father's untimely death from tuberculosis in July 1941. Due to the Nazi occupation of Czechoslovakia and the turmoil of war throughout Europe, Boija had no other choice but to take Bea west to America, where neither of them had ever traveled before.

In the fall of 1941, after a train ride across Europe that included a bout with whooping cough, Bea and her mother boarded a transatlantic passenger ship from Lisbon to New York. Like so many immigrants before and after, they sailed past the Statue of Liberty and entered the United States at Ellis Island. They took a train to Washington, D.C., where Mac's father lived.

Within a few weeks, it became apparent that her father-in-law's house was not a suitable living arrangement. Boija found a job as a translator and moved Bea into their own apartment. An ocean away from their family in Prague and ostracized for their Eastern European accents, they began their new life in the nation's capital in December 1941, just as Bea turned 11 years old and America entered WWII.

The Making of Mr. Holston

My grandfather, William J. Holston, grew up in Lynchburg, Virginia, as both a music maker and a boat lover. He was known for tooling around in boats and making mischief on the James River—often against his mother's wishes. In one letter, a longtime family friend remarked to Bill, "You seem to have been born with boats in your heart."

Born in 1930, young Bill grew up enduring many pitfalls of the Great Depression. His father was a traveling grocery salesman who was gone during the week, leaving his mother home to work as a cashier and care for the household.

While many friends and relatives were away serving in the war, Bill was running a paper route and playing in a band, both of which he prioritized over schoolwork. He became proficient in playing many instruments, including the piano, saxophone, and trumpet, as well as composing musical arrangements.

In October 1948, after a few semesters at Lynchburg College, Bill enlisted in the Navy, having passed the examinations that earned him a coveted spot at the Navy School of Music. His service began with recruit training in Great Lakes,

Illinois, then continued to Washington, where he trained with the U.S. Navy Band.

For the remainder of his life, Bill remained a philosopher, a music maker, and a boat lover. Perhaps that's why it seems particularly fitting that his pursuit of music and naval service ultimately guided his path to Bea.

With you at my side

The exact timeline of how the couple met and began dating remains in question. Navy documents, letters, and family folklore have revealed what is known.

In 1949, while Bill was attending Music School in Washington, D.C., Bea and Bill met through mutual friends. During that season, Bea finished business school, worked as a bookkeeper, and lived at a YWCA residence near the Capitol. Her mother, Boija, had remarried and lived nearby.

As the long-told story goes, Bill was going on dates with Bea's roommate, but the girl was never ready on time (or perhaps she wished to make him wait). The roommate would ask Bea to go downstairs to the lobby and visit with Bill for a short while until his date could make her debut.

Eventually, Bill realized he enjoyed visiting with Bea more than with the roommate. Their casual conversations in the

YWCA lobby lit a spark that would glow for more than 60 years.

In June 1950, Bill wrote Bea a first letter, most likely sent from his duty station in Norfolk, Virginia, where he was stationed on the *Midway*. According to the ship's timeline, the aircraft carrier would have just returned from a months-long deployment through the Mediterranean. During that tour, the bands Bill was part of played for military officials and foreign dignitaries in ports from Gibraltar to Turkey.

In November 1950, Bill returned from a four-month tour on the *Midway* with big plans. Borrowing cash from his parents, he bought a used car and put a down payment on an Airstream trailer. He called Bea from Norfolk and invited her to meet his family in Lynchburg. From here, their relationship sailed full speed ahead.

On April 7, 1951, Beatrice Estelle McGlasson and William Joseph Holston exchanged vows with their families present at a Methodist church near Washington, D.C. Following the small celebration, the couple honeymooned near Shenandoah National Park.

Bea joined Bill in Norfolk, where they attempted to park their trailer in his sister's backyard. A neighbor complained, which sent them to Simpson's Trailer Park, the site of their first home and address together.

After six weeks of settling in to married life, the USS *Midway* went underway to the Caribbean, forcing Bill to say a tearful goodbye to his beloved bride.

"As we said in front of God some 7 weeks ago—'I will love you in sickness and in health, for richer for poorer until death do us part—and even thereunto.' I never more sincerely meant anything in my life."

Bill Holston, May 1951, USS *Midway*

Chapter 3

Letter Transcription

In the letters that follow, this handwritten story of Bea and Bill Holston unfolds for us once more. When the letters were written, the Korean War was nearing a stalemate, the Cold War loomed, and President Harry S. Truman was serving his second term. A first-class postage stamp cost three cents, and gas was $0.27 a gallon.

As this journey aboard the USS *Midway* gets underway, I would like to share a few details about how my grandfather's letters were transcribed. As each sentence was copied from page to word processor, the original content and context were kept intact, including Bill's occasionally incorrect spelling and punctuation.

A few words were indecipherable or determined to be slang and are noted as such. Not all letters were dated, in which case the postmark date from the envelope is noted. In many cases, the corresponding weekday was added for context.

The letters are ordered chronologically as written, regardless of postmark date. Editor's notes at the end of each chapter expand on details about the people, places, and naval terminology mentioned. Whenever outside sources were consulted, those are referenced.

As you'll no doubt come to see, these letters mean so much to me and to my family, which is why I am both thrilled and humbled to share them. Whether or not you knew Bea and Bill Holston, their sweet correspondence reveals the struggles of a young Navy couple carving out their first years of life together in post-WWII America as war threatened again from both the east and west. Written from the meager quarters of an enlisted sailor's bunkroom, Bill's stories reveal insight into daily ship life aboard the USS *Midway* and share a closer look at the nuances of membership in the Navy Band.

Perhaps, though, the lasting gift of these letters is the innocence of young love still pulsing from its pages all these decades later. In a digital world that paces from one jarring headline to the next, it is my wish that the honest and raw love in these handwritten letters offers a heartwarming escape to all who stumble upon them.

And so, I hope you enjoy this treasured collection and the love story of two devoted hearts—William J. Holston and his dearest Bea.

Chapter 4

Underway: May — July 1951

USS Midway, *Norfolk, Va., 1949. Edgar T. Brown Local History Archive, Francis C. Pogue Collection, Virginia Beach Public Library*

Written off the coast of Florida on the way to Cuba

Thursday, May 24, 1951

Dearest Darling,

They are closing the mail tonight so I must get this in. Mr. Glass has done another song and I'm working on it now. I just finished an original one I wrote myself. It was a medium jump tune and sounded real great. I want to do a good or rather excellent job on Beau's because he is going to send it to New York and try to get some band there to play it. I think I'll get him to sign an exclusive contract with me. Might lead to some good money someday.

The weather is really hot now. It is very sultry and sticky. You can just feel the salt in the air. We pull in tomorrow morning sometime. It will be nice to see land again. Tomorrow night we are to play an officer's club dance. What a day that's going to be.

We've been having all kinds of drills for the past week we've been out. All in all, though it hasn't been too bad. We had it better the last cruise.

Man, I sure do miss you. I think of you constantly and am only living for the time that I can be sure that I'll <u>never</u> have to leave you again. They'll have to come and get me the next time. Oh, baby, I love you so much and while I may not be able to give you all the material luxuries of life, I can give you my love, undying and unending, and try to be a good husband.

You've been everything a wife should be and more. I appreciate all the little things you do for me so much like having my clothes laid out for me, etc. I want you to know that since I've been married I've been much happier than at any other time. You're everything I ever dreamed about... and more. You're now what makes me tick, what makes the flowers bloom and the grass grow. Without you life is a complete harsh discord.... with you, a beautiful symphony to rival the greatest of all symphonies.

Someday, there <u>shall</u> be an end to this senselessness of humanity... when man can once again live in hope and confidence with his loved ones. When young people can plan their lives and live according to the rule. Until that time, however, there will be heartache, sorrow, tears, sweat, toil... let's hope that day of peace is not too far off. As long as you love me I can undergo anything—physical or mental—that that man has created. As we said in front of God some 7 weeks ago—"I will love you in sickness and in health, for richer for poorer until death do us part—and even thereunto." I never more sincerely meant anything in my life.

Well, honey, how is your new job? I hope you like it and you are getting along O.K. By the way, I'm going to send all the mail to the trailer. Well honey that's about all from here. Pardon the pencil but I broke that 25c pen. It fell on the floor (not deck* mind you). I'm still trying to convince those cats that I'm no sailor. I'm a family man. I love you my darling— 'til the end of time—

Yours forever,
Bill

---

* On Navy ships, floors are referred to as decks. Bill's refusal to call the floor "the deck" here illustrates his tendency to rebel against authority. Later in his career as a high school principal, similar tendencies pushed him to leave the public school system and start his own private school, the Pensacola School of Liberal Arts, which he and Bea operated together for more than 40 years.

Guantanamo Bay, Cuba

Postmark: May 31, 1951

My Dearest Bea,

> *Three beautiful letters arrived today and I gladly received them. 7 days seems like so short a time but this last 7 days has really dragged by.*

> *We docked here Sat. morning and the dance band got off the ship at 1:00 to play at the Officers Club.*

> *Everything you've ever heard about the tropics and Cuba is true. It is certainly beautiful. The green foliage against the blue sky and grey mountains are simply out of this world. Guantanamo Bay is a manmade Paradise. They have terrific food and every kind of recreational facility available anywhere. Softball courts, tennis courts, ping-pong, pool, swimming, both ocean and fresh water, horseback riding and so forth.*

> *The base is really a huge playground. It is designed for the enjoyment of the forces afloat and much to my amazement this cruise is really part of a pleasure cruise. They have a 4 league softball outfit on here and practically everyone is playing in it.*

> *I sunbathed an hour yesterday and about got burned. I stayed out exactly the right time. I am the only member of the band that isn't sunburned. I'm getting mine gradually. This Cuban sun is terrifically hot.*

> *The bay here is infested with sharks. You can see them traveling in schools and breaking the water with their backs. That's the reason for the shark nets at the swimming beach.*

14

Don and I are going to go ashore to eat some delicious food. It is cheap and the greatest except for that cooked by my darling wife.

Say honey if you get time could you have the Va. Pilots* sent to me? Sure would be nice.

Those letters really made me feel great. See it's nice to have the greatest wife in existence. I sure miss you, honey. I can hardly wait til this tub pulls into Norfolk. We may get some leave, if we do, we'll spend some time at Shenandoah River Lodge†, just you and me!!

Well, my darling, I'm glad you're feeling O.K. Tell Peg and Jay‡ that I think they are the greatest people that ever lived. It's a great pleasure to be related to such fine people. I'm indeed grateful to them for everything.

Goodbye, my darling. I love you, a love that grows stronger every day. A love that will grow beyond the twilight of this life.

> *All My Love,*
> *Bill*

---

* Va. Pilot refers to *The Virginia Pilot*, Norfolk's local newspaper, which is still in circulation in print and digitally. (pilotonline.com)

† The Shenandoah River Lodge, now called the Shenandoah River Cabins, is located in Luray, Virginia, one of the gateway towns to Shenandoah National Park. (river-cabins.com)

‡ Peg (or Peggy) is Bill's older sister and only sibling. Peggy's husband, Jay Tashner, served in the Navy, survived the Pearl Harbor attacks, and was Bill's best man in their wedding. He retired as a Chief Petty Officer. Twice he turned down promotions to Warrant Officer due to the intensity of WWII and for family reasons.

Guantanamo Bay, Cuba

Postmark: Friday, May 25, 1951[*]

Dearest Darling,

The time seems to be dragging by. The last cruise didn't seem to be nearly as long. But I'm going to go out for the ship's tennis team and between that, music, and ping pong, I'll have my hands full.

I have been working quite a bit on Beau's latest song. Sometimes I feel a little lazy but I always drive myself back to work. There's too much to learn. I don't see how the boys in the band can just loaf and not do anything constructive. Some say they're going to be band directors, but they never practice or study, they only loaf around. I can't understand that.

Yesterday I went ashore for the second time. I played ping-pong for quite a while with an excellent player. I had a delicious steak. It covered the entire steak platter. That's the best food I've had since my darling wife cooked my "last meal" for me. They should have you on here as chief chef. Let's face it, you're the greatest. I hope that someday we will be able to visit Cuba or Puerto Rico. Maybe then I'll really appreciate it. At the present, the only thing I'm aware of is the fact that it is keeping me away from you.

I hope you could make it to Lynchburg[†] this last weekend. It would be nice for you to have a change of scenery.

---

[*] Based on its contents, this letter was written after the letter postmarked May 31st, indicating some sort of delay with the mail. For chronology, the letter is included in the order written.

[†] Lynchburg, Bill's hometown, is approximately 190 miles from Norfolk.

The rumor is quite prevalent that we'll be having leave parties when we get back. If so I'll probably be getting 10-15 days. And, I just want to look at you and your ravishing beauty and tell you how much I love you!! Man it is such a great feeling to know that I'm coming home to my wife instead of my girlfriend. This is quite different than the last cruise, eh? So much has happened since then. In just 11 short months since the first letter I wrote you we've been married, a newer auto, we have a home and an entirely new wonderful life has opened. Seems hard to believe that one's life can undergo such a radical change in so short a time, doesn't it?

The "Roosevelt" is going back to the "Med" in September and we are supposed to go next January. I hope I'm off of here by then.

I want to write your mom and dad a letter. Also Rene and Jack†, but, like you told me, I can only seem to want to write you. I'm going to write Luke, too, but being without a pen is a definite handicap. I think I'll try to acquire one at the Ship's Store.*

We come into the harbor practically every night. By the way, I got three letters the first time both air mail and regular mail mixed. So, I don't think there is much difference. Don't worry if you're too busy or too tired to write. I haven't been able to

---

* "Dad" here refers to Bea's stepfather. Bea's father passed away from tuberculosis in Switzerland in July 1941, which prompted the relocation with her mother to Washington, D.C. later that year.
† When Bea was 15 years old, her mother faced complications from tuberculosis and required full-time treatment in a sanatorium to recover. Having no suitable local family, her mother reached out to their former neighbors Rene and Jack Gustin, a younger couple that had moved to Buffalo, N.Y. Bea lived with the Gustins in New York for several years, finishing high school under their care while her mother thankfully recovered and lived on to meet three granddaughters and a great-grandchild (my sister).

write but about once every two days but I'm going to try to make it every day. The trouble is, except when I go ashore the same thing happens. But, please don't feel bad if you miss some days. I love and adore you just the same.

Well, my darling, I'll have to leave in a few minutes to go to General Quarters. I'll be so glad when this phase of my life is over and I won't have to be away anymore. I'm greatly antici-pating the schooling and learning that's ahead. The worry, hard work, sorrow, joy and sweat that it will take to reach my goal but with you at my side and you as my inspiration, it will be as easy as rolling off a log. I love you very much, my darling. I always shall, as long as there is life itself.

I'll be seeing you soon. Please don't work too hard. I'll be crossing my fingers hoping you'll get a transfer.

All My Love,
Your Bill

June 4, 1951
Monday morning

My Dearest Darling,

> *Well we're out at sea again after a very nice weekend. We had a dance job Friday night at the civic auditorium so we left the ship at 12:30 to go over. We went swimming, played tennis, softball and ping pong. The dance started at 8:00 and the auditorium was a large building with screened terraces, etc. The people appreciated our music very much and the members of the other band on the base were present.*

> *So we managed to big deal* staying on the beach that night. Practically everyone in the band was high, also all the dancers. The community there is very nice. The grass is very green and beautiful, on one side is a mountain and the other is the ocean. I would imagine the people would get tired of being on a playground for two years.*

> *We slept at the band barracks that night and had some very delicious food there. Those musicians play ½ minute a day. They only play colors in the morning and that's all. The rest of the day is theirs. They have every form of recreation imaginable on the base. So after breakfast I played tennis for a while then ping pong the rest of the day. We had a steak dinner for free at the chief's club and played there from 8-11:30. Man were they drunk! I've never seen a more drunk bunch of people.*

---

* "Big deal" is a slang term. It is also used again in the letter dated January 20, 1952.

They just had mail call so perhaps I'll have another letter from you!!!

So, after we played at the chief's club we went back to the band barracks and spent Sat. night there.

Sunday I spent half the day on the tennis court and I got my arms slightly burned. You can't imagine how hot that sun is. You can get burned in a half hour. It's brutal around 2:00.

So after whiling away the rest of the day I came back to the ship. Man were those sailors drunk. They behaved like a bunch of animals. One boy wanted to fight anything and everybody. This morning I'm pretty sore. Every muscle in my body is complaining. Also my arms burn a little but I'll feel all right in a day or so. I'm going upstairs now to see if any mail is there.

Just think, three letters for me! You precious thing you. Gee what a great feeling.

I think I may get leave when we get back to Norfolk. If I do we can spend at least a weekend at Shennandoah R.L. We can take up where we left off. I would be having such a terrific time now if only you were here. But since you came into my life it doesn't make sense without you. All these things I'm doing now will be the same things we'll do at Shennandoah R.L. but what a difference there will be!

I'm glad you've had no more ailments lately. You can't imagine how helpless I feel when you're sick.

Tuesday—

When I wrote the preceding news I wasn't feeling well at all. The sun literally saps the energy from you. I went to sleep at

4:00 yesterday and slept til 6:00 this morning. Imagine—14 hours. But needed all of it. I don't think anyone ever got a sweeter letter than the one I got from you after you received my first letter. It was a real classic!!

Rumor has it that we are leaving here July 4th for Norva*—I do know it'll be near there. We'll get in about the 10-12 of July.

We are supposed to go to Hatie soon. It seems strange to be going to all the countries you have heard about. Cuba, Jamaica, Haiti.

You know honey all I want to do is just look at you when I get home. I want to tell you you're the sweetest most beautiful, most wonderful, amiable, amorous, cookingest wife a man ever had. In short, I adore you!!!

Keep your fingers crossed and hope I can get out in October. I would really like to have that happen.

Oh, by the way, the oil in the engine was both low and needed changing. Please tell Peg that. It's perfectly O.K. for her to drive it but tell her to watch the oil!!

I am indeed sorry about Grandmother but if and when she goes she'll be much happier with her loved ones she'll be joining— wherever that may be. She'll be leaving behind all the puny actions and thoughts of mere mankind and entering a world of peace and love of fellow man—not wars and hypocrisy.

Well, my loving wife, I must close now. Lights out in a minute.

---

* **"Norva" refers to Norfolk, VA."*

I'm living for the day when I can see those sparkling eyelashes and say simply, "I love you,"

All my love,
Bill

The following letters were likely written off the coast of Jamaica.

Sunday, June 10, 1951

My Dearest Bea,

> *Yesterday was a very nice day. We came over to the shore**
> *Friday night to play a dance and we slept at the band barracks.*
> *Saturday morning I met a member of the other band who said*
> *he played tennis so, after I procured some tennis shoes and a*
> *swimming suit, we went to the tennis court. We played an*
> *hour and a half, then we went swimming, grabbed a bite to eat*
> *and then played some good games of ping-pong.*

> *About this time a tragedy occurred on the waterfront. An oiler*
> *blew up and killed several persons and seriously injured several*
> *more. We could see the flames, which were 100 ft. high. An*
> *immense cloud of smoke was drifting high into the air. It was a*
> *tragic occurrence.*

> *We then played tennis for another hour and a half before we*
> *quit. We then went bowling ten pins and for the first time at*
> *ten pins I bowled 150! Not bad, eh?*

> *Then we contemplated the long walk back to the barracks.*
> *Back here at last, I heard that all the dances were cancelled*
> *because of the accident. So I went to supper which was out of*
> *this world. I might add that here the personnel are allowed*
> *$90.00 per person per month for food and on the Midway*
> *$31.50 per month. They have steak and eggs 3 times a week in*

---

* It is uncertain where Bill is referring to. He might be writing from Jamaica, which he mentioned in his previous letters and didn't specifically mention again.

23

*the morning. Yesterday they had poached eggs for breakfast!!
We had roast beef, potatoes that were delicious, all the ice
cream we could possibly hold etc. I had two heaping trays of
everything. Man I would really put on the weight if I were
stationed here.*

*This morning they had a delicious breakfast. Fried eggs, choice
of oatmeal or dry cereal, doughnuts, buns, coffee or cocoa,
oranges, apples, or grapefruit and pineapple, tomato or orange
juice! Man these people are really in paradise!!*

*Bob, the boy that I played tennis with, is a fine person. He is
26 and has only been married 9 months himself. He is from
Boston and is a reserve. He is a great person. We went to the
show last night, which is constructed like an amphitheatre. A
funny thing happened. They have this truck filled with D. D.
I.* and 4-5 minutes before the movie, they spray the entire
area. The spray practically stifles you for a few minutes, but
after that there are no insects of any kind. This happens every
night and in a way is comical.*

*Today I'm going to play some more tennis. I warn you, I am
going to be very black when I get back. The sun is <u>hot</u>!*

*We'll have to go to the beach quite a bit when I get back. We
can go fishing, swimming, crabbing and just plain loafing.
That trip to Shennandoah R.L. still sounds the end!! Just the
two of us. Won't that be fine? I like that part better than the*

---

* D.D.I. likely refers to the chemical now known as DDT, a synthetic pesti-
cide developed in the 1940s and used widely by the military to control the
spread of malaria and other insect-borne illnesses. The use of DDT was regu-
lated in the 1950s and 60s and discontinued in the 1970s after it was deemed
harmful to humans and the environment. It is still used in some parts of the
world.   (epa.gov/ingredients-used-pesticide-products/ddt-brief-history-and-
status).

trip. If we can't get reservations, maybe we can go to some other place, huh. I just want to be with you, honey.

Beau said that there is a 50-50 chance I may get out. Oh, man, wouldn't that be the end? I hope to hear from the colleges soon. I hope I can get the information I want.

Well, my darling, I have to eat again. You look forward to eating around here.

We're supposed to get to Norva either the 9th or 10th of July. I sure am going to be on pins and needles 'til I have you in my arms again. It seems like such a long time, doesn't it?

I love you honey, more every day. You've certainly given me everything a woman ever could give a man. In military terms they would say—above and beyond the call of duty.

Goodbye, darling, until I can again be with you. I shall only be half a man, what with part of me in Norfolk.

All My Love Forever,
Bill

Jamaica

Tuesday, June 12, 1951

My Dearest Darling,

> *I got three more letters from you today. One told about Grandma's death* for which I am indeed very sorry. But I know wherever she is now that she is happy.*
>
> *I was infuriated at reading about Simpson and the electricity. Evidently all the stories we heard were true.*
>
> *I sure do miss you, honey. This cruise has been so much harder than the last one to the Med. All I want to do now is go home and live with you in a normal life, not floating around on some warship. I have never been moody before in my life until this cruise! But there are some people I just don't have anything to do with. We have some babies and just plain kids in the band. If a person can live 24 hours a day with a band of musicians and get along with them, then he's O.K.*
>
> *I wrote the University of Chicago and Tulane yesterday while I was waiting for the mail to close. The mail leaves the ship on Friday and Monday. So the letters should arrive about 5-6 days between. This mail situation is all fouled up though. I*

---

* Bill's maternal grandmother, Sadie Adelaide Stilphen Harkness, passed away on May 31, 1951, at age 88. At Bea and Bill's wedding weeks earlier, Sadie passed down her parents' wedding ring, inscribed "John to Sadie 1869" for Bea to wear. This simple but cherished gold band became Bea's wedding ring.

On my wedding day to my husband, Nick, in 2005, Bea loaned me the ring as my something old and something borrowed. She told me she wasn't ready to part with it yet. After she passed away, I reluctantly accepted the ring. When Nick and I found out we were expecting a daughter, we named her Sadie. Our Sadie will one day inherit the heirloom ring.

*don't know where you ever got the idea I was intending
playing in nightclubs for a living, honey. I wouldn't have that
on a silver platter. I want to have one of the best educations
possible and then be a 'lil 'old band director or professor of
Harmony and theory. Also I might be able to do arrangements
for dance bands but I never want to play in them. I dislike
playing in this one. No, baby, when night comes I just want to
turn on the radio, take off my shoes (and use those new
bedroom slippers) and hold you in my arms and tell you that
you're about the most beautiful creature that God ever made!!
Every summer we can go to teachers conventions and have
plenty of diversion so we don't get into a humdrum pattern.
Just think, people will call me Mr. Holston!!!*

*But seriously, the days are just dragging by. I miss you so much
honey. It's going to be great seeing you again. I don't ever want
to leave you again. I hate this navy and all it stands for. I
realize that it's going to be tough when I get out. I'll probably
have to work at night and study in the day, but it'll be worth
all the hardships to attain the goal I've made for myself.*

*I hope you won't have to work anymore after I get out of the
Navy*, but you can never tell. One advantage I'll have though
is that so many people are in the services for 4 years that I'll be
able to pick up temporary work while I'm studying, however,
we'll worry about those things when they happen, eh?*

*I'm looking forward to our weekend at Shenandoah River
Lodge. I just want to look at you Mrs. Holston!!*

*Everyone here is holding his breath concerning the extension of
the enlistments. Man I don't see how these young guys coming*

---

* This particular hope amounted to wishful thinking. Bea ran the office at
the School of Liberal Arts well into her 70s.

27

*in can stand to know they are joining for 4 years! That would
be too much for me.*

*Well honey, I must go to General Quarters. I'll finish this when
I get back.*

At sea between Jamaica and Haiti

Wed, June 13, 1951

*Seems like I didn't get back as soon as I intended, honey. The
time has flown by since last Friday. I wrote you Sunday from
the barracks ashore. As you gathered from my preceding letter,
I spent the entire weekend ashore. They really live like kings
there.*

*We have been having a rather strenuous time lately. They are
having General Quarters every day and tomorrow it lasts from
8:00 to 12:00. That is really a big drag.*

*The life when we're out is quite dull and unexciting. We do the
same thing every day. It's only when we get into the port that
anything interesting happens.*

*I am still hoping that I'll be able to get out of the Navy in
October. So far, nothing has happened by way of Congress. It
seems unthinkable that they would let us out and keep the
extended persons in, but the Service does the unexpected
frequently.*

*Man, I can't tell you how much I want to be home with you. I
can't see how anyone can ever stay in the Navy 20 years when
he has a family. My whole life, from the moment I married
you, became you. You figure in everything I think, say or do. To*

be away for 1-6 months at a stretch is something I just don't enjoy at all. I want to spend all of my days with you when I'm out of this outfit. Just you, me, and our children.

Bob must wonder what kind of person you are because every other word was "Bea" or "my wife." I just wouldn't even let him talk about his wife. I do seriously believe that I have the most perfect person that God ever made! And, Mrs. Holston, I have quite a few people who will back me on that!!

Don't worry about me taking leave. I am going to make all my plans to suit your job. We will take a little weekend vacation to Shennandoah River Lodge, though, won't we? Just the two of us together. By the way, I wrote your mother a little note and invited her down for a few days. Hope she and Bill can make it.

Well, honey, suppertime!! Gotta get healthy, my better half ordered me to you know... I love you my darling and I'll be in Utopia when my arms can once again hold you.

All My Love,
Bill

At sea, heading to Port Au Prince, Haiti

Friday, June 15, 1951

My Dearest Darling,

I just returned from an excellent movie named "Toast of New Orleans."* It made me homesick though… homesick for you and for our life together. This cruise has been an extremely trying one on me compared to the Med cruise. I am living only for the time I again can be home and we can resume our life where we left off. I miss you something terrible, darling, at nighttime I long to feel you with me but all I see is a disgusting Naval Bunk. We have so much to do… together.

Every night I relive the memories of our life together. I can still see you coming down the aisle… no saint or angel could have ever matched your poise and looks. You were the very essence of purity and all things good in the world. For a few brief days, the world and all its puny meanings and man's mad passions and desires were left behind and we were floating on a celestial cloud and basking in the light of those who had just begun to taste the nectar of life… I think we learned that there is much more to life than money and the mad perpetual scramble for it… the things that really count are the simple things of which everyone can benefit. I may not be able to bestow upon you the greatest material wealth, but I am going to try to be the greatest husband. You are so perfect and sweet. Darling I realize how fortunate I am. Everyone who has ever met you has sung your praises. As I once said before, someday there will be

---

* Set in the year 1905, *The Toast of New Orleans* (1950) is a musical about a Louisiana bayou fisherman who falls in love with an opera singer. It likely appealed to Shoopa because of the combination of boats and music. (imdb.-com/title/tt0043053/)

an end to this fighting and I'll be able to return home and be
with you, never to leave again.

We're docking at Port Au Prince, Haiti, tomorrow. It is a fine
liberty port. Listen to its qualifications: 60 (sixty) percent of
the population has syphilis. The water and food are all conta-
minated. You can contact yaws, a form of venereal disease by
flies and mosquitoes lighting on an open wound or sore. The
venereal disease here takes months of constant medications to
cure. So you can see that it is the worst. But we have a dance
job at the Officers Club tomorrow night so I'll have to go. I
want to play some tennis late in the afternoon and the Officers
Club is two miles from town so maybe it wont be too bad. It's
sort of like the American Club they have outside Athens. *

We have five replacements on the way from Music School.† I
heard some excellent news from the chief today too. He seems
to think the leading idea now is to let out the reserves and men
whose enlistments are going to expire for the first time (in
other words I'll get out in October). Man if that only
happens… but I'm trying not to get too excited over it.

The Captain made a little speech tonight and said we have
exactly three more weeks here before we leave. Man, three
weeks from now we'll be heading home!!!!!

---

* According to the *Mediterranean Cruise Book*, the port call locations during
the USS *Midway's* 1950 cruise were Gibraltar, Sicily, Naples, Tunisia, Cypress,
Istanbul, Athens, Suda Bay, Malta, Palermo, Cannes, Algeria, and Lisbon. Bill
references this busy deployment, often in contrast to the monotony of the
current underways. (navysite.de/cruisebooks/cv41-50/index.html)

† In 1951, the Naval School of Music was located in Washington, D.C. At the
time, musicians trained together, graduated as an ensemble, and served
together at a naval installation. A larger Navy music school, serving musicians
from the Marines and Army, opened in Virginia Beach in the 1960s.

(netc.navy.mil/Commands/Center-for-Service-Support/Naval-School-of-
Music/History/)

Well, honey, I'm getting very sleepy and tomorrow is a stren-
uous day so I must close. I love you, my dear, soon we'll be
together again and we can obliviate ourselves to the world and
dwell together in paradise.

All My Love Forever,
Bill

Port Au Prince, Haiti

Monday, June 18, 1951

My Dearest Darling,

*What a weekend we had. We got practically no sleep but we
had a terrific time. Saturday we left the ships at 12:00 and we
went to the American Embassy. We had a dance job at the
American Embassy Club starting at 8:00 so we were their
guests and everything was on the house. The club was modern
with a nice golf course, swimming pool, tennis court and situ-
ated at the foot of a 3500-foot mountain. There were only a
few officers there so we had an enjoyable time. We went swimming and ate and drank all afternoon.*

*We had no certain time to quiet… we were to be told "when"
by the Executive Officer. So we started at 8:00 and played
until 2:00 in the morning. That's the first time I've played a 6-
hour dance in my life. We got back to the ship at 4:00 A.M.
The Club had promised to give us a free trip or tour the next
day (Sunday) at 11:30 so we had to get up at 8:00 to leave
the ship at 10:30. We met the owner of the club and he
assigned us the various cars. All the cars here are brand new
American cars by the way. We were driven to the top of the
3500 ft. mountain and the view was appalling.* The town
was at the base and the sea extended as far as one could see.
We then went back down to the city and went to a club called
the El Rancho Grande and we dug a Haitian Jam Session. That
was the weirdest. They really put everything into their music.
Then we were driven to another club. The natives were putting*

---

* "Appalling" is transcribed as written. It is uncertain if this is slang or
sarcasm or whether he meant to describe the view as appealing. He later
describes the mountaintop view as "out of this world."

on an ancient ritual and it was something to see. They were dressed in bright colors and dancing to a small dance orchestra. We then went to the mahogany factory. It was there that I went berserk. Everything was so beautiful and I only had $5.50. I hunted and hunted and finally found the items I wanted. They are beautiful and I hope you will like them. Everything I got is practical. I'll let you guess as to what I got. After the mahogany factory we went to this beautiful hotel up in the mountains to eat. The view was out of this world. On one side the mountains were prominent… on the other side the ocean. The hotel is not completely finished and already it has cost $100,000. The swimming pool alone cost $12,000 and is not yet completed. We had a six-course dinner after talking with the receptionist. We five were the only ones there. We had soup, lobster, chicken, vegetables, 8 different kinds of cheeses, salad, ice cream and after dinner coffee, and several items I have forgotten. When we came to the dock to await the chief and the mastersergent we had left the night before. Then I had some fun. The natives went crazy over that old watch I had. They wanted to trade me a lot of stuff for it. One kid has a jeweled one he said I could have for $10 because he's getting another soon. So I traded that watch I got in Palermo a year ago (I payed $10) for $20.00 worth of mahogany items. I have everything we'll ever need for the trailer. I'll still let you wonder but I know you'll be pleased.

We're supposed to get from 7-14 days when we get back. If you're thinking of quitting why not wait 'til I get home. We could have several weeks together then. I'm not certain how long our leave will be but since I have so much saved I may as well take it. I hope you can get a job at the Air Station. Why not call about it. Oh well, I know you're better in situations like this than I. If we have the weekend off together we'll go to D. C. or any place you wish. I'll merely be your meek servant and your every wish will be my command.

If we do have a week off I know of one place I would like to go for two days… but we'll wait to see what happens.

Do you remember Ensign Beechnut (?) in the play? He just got discharged. Perhaps they're getting more lenient now. The consensus aboard ship is that I'll get out. Let's hope so. Mr. Beechnut who is really a J.G. * *is going to the University of Virginia. Man, that's the end. He'll probably be a freshman to boot.*

When I get home honey, we're going to play tennis, go on picnics, go swimming and just plain old have a great time. It won't be too much longer now.

Goodbye, darling, I'll be so glad to be back to you and our home. Thank you for being such a great wife.

All My Love,
Bill

---

* J.G. refers to the Navy rank Lieutenant Junior Grade, the second lowest officer ranking in the Navy.

At sea between Haiti and Puerto Rico

Thursday, June 28, 1951

Dearest Darling,

Well, honey, the days are slowly but surely dwindling away. It won't be too much longer now 'til we're together again. This cruise has been much worse than the cruise to the Mediterranean last year.* There is nothing to see here except sailors and I see my share of those on the ship. I think you will like the mahogany I got in Haiti. We have enough to furnish the entire trailer! That is the only change we've had since we've been here.

I have been very sick, the last few days with terrible stomach cramps. About one-half the ship is laid up. The food on the tub gets worse every day. They're passing the buck from one person to another as to who is to blame for the food poisoning. Man I really did have terrible pains for awhile.

We're going to Culebra† this weekend. I don't know where that is but I understand there's nothing there. I'll have to finish this letter honey, this pen is writing too bad to continue. I'll finish this as soon as I get hold of a decent one.

I have leave from July 11 to July 29 so I want to do everything to make you happy. We can go to Lynchburg, Washington or that little hotel at Chesapeake Beach. It would be nice to go to

---

* The USS *Midway* cruise to the Mediterranean in 1950, included 14 stops in nearly a dozen different countries in Europe, Africa, and Asia. By comparison, Bill's follow-on tour to the Caribbean was notably underwhelming.

† Culebra is a deep port city on the Isla de Culebra, which is part of Puerto Rico. Karl Zingheim at the USS Midway Museum explained the small island was a bombing range off Puerto Rico used by the fleet until 1975.

Washington soon after the ship comes in. I would like to see your mother and father and take you to the Cafe of All Nations* (I haven't gotten you there yet.) We might make reservations for one weekend at Shennandoah River Lodge – we must go there this summer.

The only thing on my mind now is going home. Some time I think about my life before we were married and I wonder how I ever enjoyed myself. I had nothing to look forward to and nothing definite to work for. But, my darling, everything is as plain as can be now, thanks to you. Mother told me in her last letter how fortunate I was to have such a fine lady for a wife (as if I didn't know). The whole family is crazy about you, honey. I'm so glad it's that way. So many people are having a tough time because of in-law trouble. By the way, we are invited to a wedding the 22nd of July. Just think, our first since April 7th!

Well, honey, mail closes in a few minutes. I want to be sure to get this in. Just think, less than two weeks 'til I get home. I'll be dreaming about you, darling. I love you so much.

All my love,
Bill

P.S. I love you---

P.S. Jr. I am enclosing your dependents card, honey. I was finally able to get it.

---

* The Cafe of All Nations was a popular restaurant attached to the Mayflower Hotel in Washington, D.C. It was known among the young, Navy crowd for having affordable drinks and live music.

Friday, June 29, 1951

My Dearest Darling,

*Today we had a mail call and I got 1 from mother, one from
your mother and 2 from you!! Gee it was great hearing from
you and I was very pleased Rene & Jack liked the trailer. I
think your quitting work was a good idea. I don't want you to
be unhappy in the least and as long as you have to work it
might as well be in pleasant surroundings. Your mother wrote
a very sweet letter… we can go to Washington or any place
you like from the 12th on. I do want to spend the first night
and day in our own home… together… just the two of us.
Maybe we could go to Washington for 2-3 days then to
Lynchburg then meet Arlene* at Hungry Mother's State Park
at Marion Virginia. That's near the West Virginia border, you
know. But honey anything you plan will suite me perfectly…
the only requirement is that we be together.*

*We're almost at Culebra now. They're going to bomb and
racket† it for the next 3 days. We go on liberty at Guantanamo
July 4th and leave for home July 6th. We shall arrive probably
the 10th. My leave will start midnight to the 10th and will
expire the 29th of July. Every moment will be devoted to you.
There is one place I would like to go. Do you remember me
telling you about the state vocational tests at Danville, Va?*

---

* Arlene was one of Bea's best friends and an attendant in their wedding.
The two remained close and exchanged letters throughout their lives.

Here, Shoopa is scheming up a plan to see Bea's mom and stepfather (in
D.C.), his parents (in Lynchburg, Va.), and best friend Arlene (at the state
park near West Virginia).

† After failing to decipher the phrase "bomb and racket," the USS *Midway's*
historian, Karl Zingham, illuminated why: "Your grandfather was actually
referring to 'bomb and rocket,' as unguided rockets were used as ordnance up
through the Vietnam War era. These missions were important to give pilots
proficiency in weapons deployment."

Maybe the two of us could take them, huh. I would like to know just what my innate abilities are.

I can't tell you how I'll be looking forward to seeing you. It seems like an eternity since I last saw you at Peg's house. We'll be operating in and out until the first of 1952… that's straight dope. We have one 10-day cruise to Nova Scotia and that's all. I'm going to get a little something from each of the ports we hit for the trailer. I would like to get some curtain material from Nova Scotia, etc.

I warn you I'll be eating 6 meals a day when I'm home. The food on here has been the lousiest I've had in the Navy… especially this cruise. Every one on this ship has had the mysterious illness… I was sick for a week, and two of those days were terrible. They still haven't found the cause of the trouble.

Well honey, must go to bed now. Will write again tomorrow. I love you my darling… more than you will ever know. You are my life. Everything I do, or say has you as its impetus. I thank God every night that he gave me such a wonderful, considerate lady for my wife. When I walk those last remaining yards to the trailer door and see you inside waiting for me, I'll know just what heaven is really like… the world with its cares and tribulations will vanish and we two shall float away on a cloud to utopia. It'll be like that forever… 'til death us do part… and even thereafter.

Goodnight My Love,
Your Bill

P.S. I wrote a poem to you last night, honey. It may not be the greatest, but it does help describe you.

The sunset beyond the mountains,

39

The moonlight on the sea
Could not for an instant capture
The beauty that is thee.

For beauty is more than seeing things,
that's just a minor part.
Beauty is that which is hidden
Within the holiest heart.

If I were asked what was beauty,
My reply would instantly be
All things that are pure, holy, and lovely,
The personification of thee.

I love you my darling… July 10th is not too far away now. I'm
getting very excited. It seems like ages since my arms held you.

Goodbye Honey,
Your Bill

Chapter 5

Reflections of a Granddaughter

A hug from a grandfather.

Growing up with caring, involved grandparents is one of life's most irreplaceable gifts. Since our paternal grandmother passed away the year I was born, Bea did double duty as the only grandmother my sister and I knew.

Hindsight has made it especially clear that my grandparents were as original as the name Shoopa itself. The name was born from a mispronunciation by my sister, Courtney, when she was learning to speak as a toddler. In true Shoopa fashion, he leaned into the idea of doing things his own way, and his four grandchildren grew up calling him this unique name. There was, indeed, only one Shoopa.

Throughout my elementary school years, my dad's job in the oil industry relocated our family several times across the Midwest. No matter where we moved, Bea and Shoopa's house in Pensacola remained a home base for my sister and me. We would drive for days, if needed, to see our grandparents, aunts, and cousins at their welcoming home on Bayou Chico. Catching croaker and catfish off their dock and tooling around in Shoopa's rowboats became my favorite pastimes.

In 1991, I was eight years old and living in Oklahoma when my dad was downsized out of the oil industry. His sudden unemployment created a chance opportunity to move anywhere. There wasn't anywhere else our family wanted to be except Pensacola.

After living so far away from Bea and Shoopa, moving into a house a mile away christened a sweet new season surrounded by local family. My Aunt Jill (my mom's youngest sister) lived on the other side of Bayou Chico. My Aunt Wendy and my two cousins, Chris and Erika, were 15 minutes away in an older part of town called East Hill. Their home was right around the corner from the Holston's family home, where my mom and her sisters grew up.

Decades earlier, in 1969, Bea and Shoopa had founded the Pensacola Private School of Liberal Arts, which eventually relocated to operate out of their longtime family home in East Hill. The small, alternative school served local students from this location for more than 40 years.

Thanks to our move to Pensacola, much of my childhood overlapped with my grandparents' golden years. This season allowed me to know Bea and Shoopa, not only as family members, but as neighbors and community members.

Parents and students at the School of Liberal Arts revered Bea and Shoopa for their enthusiasm for education and flexibility accommodating individual students' needs. Shoopa's former students from the Pensacola High School (PHS) marching band kept close in touch, hosting regular reunions for decades.

Alongside running the school and maintaining an eclectic fleet of boats, Bea and Shoopa were the kind of grandparents who went out of their way to create opportunities for my cousins, my sister, and me that we wouldn't have experienced otherwise. They sent us to sailing camp and provided an endless supply of bait for fishing off the dock. They planned short getaways in their motorhome to nearby towns. They created a cozy loft on the second floor of their house where we could retreat to watch movies after family meals.

Conspiring as tour guides, entertainers, teachers, and mentors, Bea and Shoopa enriched our lives and invested in our personal interests. Together, they made our childhood magical.

When I was 16 and in my sophomore year at Pensacola High School (where Shoopa had taught as the band director), my dad accepted a new job in Houston, Texas. I can remember crying in Bea's arms about the news that we were moving away from Pensacola, her honey voice consoling me. After the move, we resumed long-distance communication with Bea and Shoopa, calling and visiting whenever possible.

During my first year of college, I invited Bea to be my pen pal. We exchanged letters for a few years, which Bea sprinkled with favorite Bible verses and treasured memories from her first years of knowing Shoopa. One of the letters contained a check for $100—airfare to attend a Navy dance with my long-distance boyfriend, Nick, who was well into his Plebe (first) year at the U.S. Naval Academy.

At some point, through visits and letters, amidst graduating from college and marrying Nick, I came to see Bea as more than a family member. She became a dear friend. And not just any friend—one who had known and loved me unconditionally since the day I was born.

But in the length of a short phone call, everything changed.

Chapter 6

Underway: October – November 1951

Unlike the previous journey to the Caribbean, the following series of letters are more difficult to track geographically. Based on the warm, summery weather referenced in one November letter, it appears the Midway again traveled south. No geographical locations are referenced, which likely indicates there were no ports of call on this cruise. For band members who love to perform, this meant nothing but practice time and small performances on board the ship, adding to the monotony and further fueling Bill's longing for home and Bea.

Atlantic Ocean off the East Coast

Postmark: Monday, October 22, 1951

Dearest Bea,

Mail closes in a few minutes so I thought I'd try to get this in to you. It was terrible seeing you drive off like that but there is some consolation in knowing I'll be home in a few weeks and not in Korea.* At the most there will only be one more long separation and that will be the last. I just want to be alone with you, the trailer, and the vacuum cleaner†. I love you my sweet, you're the sweetest thing I ever saw!!!

Be a sweet little girl while papa is away, I'm sorry I won't be there to warm you up at night times but maybe it won't be too cold while I'm gone.

I must close now, darling. I'm sure going to miss you. I don't know how I ever enjoyed life before I met you.

So long honey, see you in a couple of weeks.

All my love and devotion,
Bill

---

* According to the U.S. State Department, the Korean War began on June 25, 1950. Between July 1951, and July 1953, a stalemate ensued in which little new territory was claimed by either side. The stalemate eventually led to the July 1953, armistice that designated the 38th parallel as the new border between North and South Korea. (history.state.gov/departmenthistory/short-history/koreanwar).

† Since the discovery of these letters, Shoopa's apparent infatuation with this vacuum cleaner has become a source of great amusement within our family. Or perhaps it was an inside joke? We're not quite sure. But there are more mentions to come.

Postmark: Sunday, October 28, 1951

My Dearest Darling,

> *There is a rumor that mail is leaving tomorrow so I want to write you in case it does.*

> *The cruise has been monotonous. I don't think of time because it goes too slow. I try to do the same thing every day and that way it goes by faster. I miss you so much my darling. I never want to think of leaving home again. There is only one place for me and that is Lot No. 8*—but soon we won't have to worry anymore. I'll have 18 months when I get back home so I'll be due for transfer any time after that.*

> *I'm studying all my spare time. Symington† put me in charge of the dance band so I have my hands full. Time just won't go by fast enough, though. We do have one nice vacation from the first Wednesday in after the dance job 'til Monday morning. That falls on Thanksgiving Week, too. We'll plan to leave for Lynchburg Friday afternoon after you get off from work. Jack is going with us, you know, so we should have a good time.*

---

* Lot No. 8 is the site number their trailer was parked on at Simson's Trailer Park in Norfolk.

† Bill's band director, Arthur "Sy" Symington, was later stationed in Pensacola and retired there after a celebrated 50-year musical career with the Navy. After leaving active-duty, he was the music director of the Naval Aviation School's Command for 14 years as a civilian. Following retirement, he continued serving as a volunteer. He and Bill maintained a close local friendship

Shortly before Symington's death in 1987, the Pensacola Naval Air Station named the musical rehearsal building in his honor. At the time, it was the only building on base named after an enlisted sailor. (*The Pensacola News Journal*, archives). Bea and Bill remained close friends with Sy's widow Ethel and their extended family.

The cocoa and cheese etc. is tideing me over nicely. It feels good to go to sleep with a full stomach.

I hope everything is all right at home. Be sure to wipe that oil line often. It worries me to think of it leaking like that.

I want so much to be with you honey. I can just see your sparkling eyes. I never knew what happiness was until I married you. I've enjoyed every moment of our life together, it's simply wonderful.

There are so many pleasant memories to remember. We certainly have everything to look forward to.

Just think, when I get home I can go downtown and shop for your Christmas present!!! I'm going to set both of your Christmas and birthday presents* in the living room and let you have the best time trying to guess what might be inside. I can just see you now.

Well my darling, that's about all the news from here. Since we get no liberty until we get back, there won't be anything new or interesting happening. They have no more schedule for mail either so this may be the last news until you see my shining face in front of that beautiful Liberty door. Did I ever tell you about Liberty doors†—oh that's right. You live in one.

I won't rest until I can hold you in my arms. I have the worst time sleeping. I've been so used to having your adorable body next to mine that I just can't sleep without you. Take good care

---

* Bea's birthday was December 9th. She would have been turning 21.
† Researching the term "Liberty doors" yielded no further information. Liberty is the term used when sailors are on regular time off, such as weekends and holidays, as opposed to leave, which is earned time off. His tone here sounds sarcastic, so it's clear he was ready to take leave again.

of the trailer and vacuum cleaner for me. By the way I'm going to increase the allotment soon.

I love you my darling. Without you life would be a void of frustrations and emotions. With you life is a heaven… where only you and I reign as king and queen. Soon I'll be home again and once more, time and life will have a meaning.

All My Love,
Bill

PS. I love you—Madly—

Postmark: Friday, Nov. 2, 1951

Dearest Darling,

Lights are out, everyone is asleep, so it's time once again for me to return to you in spirit. You are the one sure thing in this whole unsure picture, the Gibraltar of my life, so to speak.* I'll be so happy to see you, honey, I miss you so much. It's just like having two lives. One is at home where I feel like I'm king of all I can see, the other where all I can see is king over me. The vastness of the ship, 4000 men, the huge body of water, all tend to belittle the individual. But, I only have to think of you and the life that is waiting for me, and I know that I'm much bigger than my environment.

All I can say, my darling, is that I love you—with a love as such no person has ever known.

My thoughts are constantly with you and I long to feel your arms around me, the goodnight kiss, and the warmth of your body. Those are the things a man spends a lifetime searching to find and I've already succeeded.

Today I received three letters from you. I felt like a new man when I read them. Just reading something you've written gives me such a thrill and your wit keeps me in stitches.

We will have 2 or three nights a week to play after I get back. Our new Executive Officer is trying to rebuild the Navy

---

* When the USS *Midway* went underway in January 1950, and again in July, its first port call was Gibraltar. By calling Bea "the Gibraltar of my life," Shoopa would have been referencing, not only the giant rock, but also the first respite port call and beacon of hope after 10 monotonous days crossing the Atlantic Ocean.

starting with the Midway. So Sy is going to make it look good on paper as far as the bands' work is concerned.

I'm still studying hard. I'm getting a lot accomplished although I hate the circumstances. I still haven't run across Mr. Byland on the ship.

You know one of the things that makes me mad is the fact that it seems I'm doing the Navy no good at all. I don't make the ship go or keep it going consequently there seems no need of me even being here.* But, who is to use logic in connection with the Navy?

I showed the cartoon to Palm and he got a laugh out of it. He told me you were a little shaky when he drove by. It will give you confidence in your driving. Why, just look who taught you!! (ahem). I'm glad it (the car) starts all right. If you drive too much have the oil changed, honey. Be sure to keep that oil line from the furnace wiped off. I worry about that catching on fire or something.

---

* Without port calls, Bill appears to have lost a sense of purpose on this cruise. But his efforts were previously recognized by leadership. On Sept. 27, 1950, Bill received a letter of commendation from Captain F. N. Kivette, Commanding Officer of the USS *Midway*. The letter illustrates the merits of the band on that tour.

1. The Commanding Officer takes great pleasure in commending you, as a member of the U.S.S. MIDWAY Band, for your exceptional performance given on the night of 30 August 1950, at the Palm Beach Casino, Cannes, France.

2. At the dinner dance given on the occasion of the awards presentation of the Motor Yacht of Cote d' Azur, your contribution to the rendition of both military and popular music was outstanding and was well received by the peoples of France and other nations present, including United States Naval Officers.

3. Your music has not only continuously brought enjoyment to embarked personnel but has added much to the prestige of the United States Navy in foreign ports.

4. This letter will be made a part of your official record and will be placed in your service record.

Well, Darling, I'm starting to get very sleepy. We've had only 16 days left but it seems like 160. It'll be so nice when I can return to our own little home and live the only life that God ever intended a man to live. I love you so much Bea. I'll never be able to tell you in words, but I hope in my deeds that you will come to have an inkling of how much. You're the greatest thing that ever happened to me, darling. I thank God for the blessed day you were born. I'll go to bed now and dream of you, of us (and the trailer).

All My Love,
Bill

P.S. I adore you. See you soon.

Saturday, Nov. 3, 1951

Dearest Bea,

Well, my darling, only 13 more days to go until I'll be home with you. They seem much longer.

We haven't done anything exciting on this whole cruise. Today I had flight quarters and I had a chance to get a little sun. I'm busy writing a theme song for the dance band and studying my Schillinger Course.* I've progressed to about page 45.

There are so many things I want to do when I get home. All I can think about is getting home to you. It seems like centuries since I last saw you and it was only 12 days ago.

One thing I do want to do when I get back is to do my Christmas shopping. I can see you now pestering me to know what's inside. I'm not going to tell you a thing either.

We had a little commotion today at flight quarters. One of the planes parked on the flight deck rolled off the edge when the ship made a sharp turn. The boy sitting inside jumped outside though. Just think, ½ a million dollars lost in one blow!

The weather here is very warm. It is just like it was in the summertime. I hope to have a nice suntan by the time we get home. They're getting pretty strict on here about uniforms though so I'll have to do it on the sly.

---

* The Schillinger Course is a mathematics-based music composition program created by Joseph Schillinger, who taught many famous musicians such as George Gershwin and Glenn Miller. The Schillinger System of Musical Composition was thought to be a tedious but effective way of composing music.

(jeremyarden.com/theschillingerschoolofmusic)

Well, my darling, there just isn't any news on this flat top. About the only real news (and it's not news, it's about 1 year old now) is that I love you intensely.

I just can't wait until I can hold you in my arms and whisper sweet words into your lovable ears. It's been so long, too long.

Soon this nightmare will end though, and we'll be together again.

Good night my darling, pleasant dreams.

All My Love,
Bill

Postmark: Nov. 5, 1951
Monday

My Dearest Bea,

Yesterday I got another letter from you. Upon my Southern honor you're the best 'lil 'ole letter writer ah ever saw. Believe me I appreciate it, too.

We played constantly yesterday afternoon from 12:30 to 5:00. We had to play for the refueling of the destroyers. The only consolation was that I did get a little suntan. The sun isn't so strong. I didn't get burned although I stayed out all day. I want to try to be nice and tanned when I get back so I'll look nice in my new clothes. You can be so proud of me.

I never did see Mac. Maybe he didn't fly the mail out after all. The letter was postmarked Norfolk???

Be sure to keep that oil line inside wiped off darling. I'm going to fix that first thing I get back.

The time is gradually running out. We have 12 days left now. We're passed the half way mark.

I had a dream last night that as soon as I got back to Norva my orders were there. I was the only one that got transferred and the other boys were mad at me because of it. Wouldn't that be a nice Christmas present??? Let's hope it's to New Orleans when I do leave.

It's hard to believe that one month from today will be Dec. 5th. It's just like summertime here so it's hard to imagine wintertime is practically here.

I haven't quite decided what to give you for Christmas. I'll just let you guess a while. Take care of yourself honey. I'm proud of you driving the car like you do. Of course you had an excellent teacher (ahem) but you learned beautifully.

The only thought on my mind is that soon I'll be home with you and the trailer (and vacuum cleaner). I love you my darling. I'm so grateful that I have you—without you life wouldn't mean a <u>thing</u>. <u>You</u>'re just the greatest little thing that ever happened to me. Goodbye my darling.

All My Love,
Bill

Thursday, Nov. 8, 1951

Dearest Darling,

What a fine day. I got 4 letters from you today. It was a wonderful experience to get news from my sweet wife. I can't tell you how much I love you darling. We were just meant to be married to each other. I hope I can give you the things I want to.

Another grotesque but amusing thing happened yesterday. Remind me to tell you when I get home.

They had a tragic accident on the small carrier with us. A plane crashed into the island and killed 14 men.

We are doing mostly dance band work, trying to get the band in shape. I'm trying to make the band sound like something— believe me that's quite a job.

I've gotten to page 60 in my Schillinger book and finished that thing for the Admiral. I have accomplished quite a bit on this cruise. I just hope I get transferred before we are supposed to go to the Med. We would be able to save probably a hundred dollars a month more. But I had much rather be home with my sweet wife any day than save even $300 a month more. Money could never give me the happiness you have given me. I have so many wonderful memories and to think that our life together has only started! We have everything to which to look forward!

The only thing that keeps us sane here is the fact that soon we'll be home. I'm glad you have nothing in particular to do when I get home. We'll just stay home for a few days. I just want to love you and love you and love you.

Well, my darling, I must be getting ready to play for the movies tonight. I hate saying goodbye but mail closes soon and I want to be sure you get this.

Be a good little girl and take care of the trailer and vacuum cleaner. In 9 days I'll be in our own little home with my own little wife. Believe me I'll be the happiest.
Goodbye my darling—'til the 17th.

All My Love,
Bill

P.S. I love and adore you.

Chapter 7

The Phone Call

2007

The phone call that changed everything came in February 2007, two days after my 24th birthday.

I was newly married to Nick, and we were living in the sunny seaside town of Coronado, California. He was a lowly ensign enduring the throes of basic training, and I was working at the American Red Cross in San Diego.

That week (as during countless others), Nick was away on a training trip—this time in Alaska. Like many birthdays to come, I was on my own to celebrate the day.

Shortly after having cake with co-workers, the phone rang at my desk. I answered it, surprised to hear Bea's familiar voice on a line where I typically heard only from strangers. But this wasn't the call that changed everything.

Bea was simply calling to wish me a happy birthday, as she had every year. She also checked to make sure I received the presents she sent. I thanked her, sharing that the box of goodies had arrived that morning. She said goodbye too quickly. I remember not wanting the call to end.

Even with my husband away, my 24th birthday was a

wonderful day. But two days later, everything changed. My mom called to tell me that Bea was in the hospital. As the facts unfolded, I overheard the unsavory phrase *pancreatic cancer*.

This was not our family's first round of cancer news. Some 15 years earlier, Shoopa had been diagnosed with prostate cancer. But Bea's diagnosis seemed instantly more troublesome.

A quick Google search revealed the details no one dared say aloud. With no treatments available at the time, 95 percent of pancreatic cancer patients died within five years of diagnosis. At 76 years old, Bea's prognosis couldn't possibly be good.

It wasn't.

A few weeks later, my mom held the phone up to Bea's thinning face. We said our final goodbyes, her honey voice speaking into my heart for the very last time.

On Tuesday, May 29, 2007, I was getting ready for work after Memorial Day weekend when I reluctantly answered the phone. I knew what my mom was calling to say. Even so, the news of Bea's passing still shattered me.

For the first time in my 24 years, I found myself in a world without Bea. Having never lost anyone so close to me before, her disappearance felt impossible to comprehend.

As the reality of the news sank further in, every part of me ached an unfamiliar kind of ache. Bea's caring presence, her voice, her letters, her calls were gone from our lives forever. I soon discovered that without this dear grandmother —the only grandmother I knew—I would no longer feel the care-freedom of childhood in the same way ever again.

Just three months after her initial diagnosis, our family gathered in Pensacola for Bea's memorial service. The pastor read Bea's favorite verses from Ecclesiastes 3 about the seasons of life under heaven.

A time to be born. And a time to die.

My cousins, Chris and Erika, and I stood at the pulpit while my sister, Courtney, offered heartfelt reflection of Bea's impact on our lives. Shoopa arranged for the pianist to perform *The Wind Beneath My Wings*. At the end of the service, the congregation sang "The Navy Hymn," a longtime favorite that Bea had requested.

When we returned to my grandparents' home after the service, Shoopa spoke words I will never forget. Standing on the dock, staring at the clouded sky above Bayou Chico, he said, "We have to move all of this into the world of memories now."

We would soon discover that entering the world of memories would bring with it a dark season—especially for Shoopa.

Chapter 8

Underway: January 1952

Atlantic Ocean, approaching Gibraltar

Friday, Jan. 18, 1952

Dearest Darling,

> *Well, honey, we're two days from Gibraltar. I'm not going off the ship on liberty except when the dance band goes ashore to possibly rehearse. I couldn't enjoy myself one bit. I keep thinking about you and how I wish I were with you and the trailer and vacuum cleaner.* Darling, I miss you terribly. I love you so much and the little while I was home I got so used to being with you that I'm like a fish out of water. I remember so well the thrill of putting my arms around you when I was there with you. There's nothing like seeing your cute, loveable nose and kissing you good night. I hope my transfer comes soon.*

> *We had a strenuous day today. I started sort of a new thing*

---

* At times it's hard to tell which Shoopa adored more ... the trailer or the vacuum cleaner.

going here. Remember how we were allowed to sleep 'til 7:
o'clock and from 10:30 A.M. to 1:00 P.M.? Well, that's all off
now throughout the ships. You shoulda heard the griping going
on. We have several saxophone players that won't practice
their parts. So I clamped down on them. I took over the sax
rehearsal and we really worked hard & slowly but surely they
started shaping up. One dance band rehearsal they fluffed off
completely so I told them to get out their horns instead of
sleeping all the time. I told Sy about it beforehand and so he
clamped down even farther. He said he would send people to
the deck division* if they didn't snap out of it. Consequently
the dance band has improved by 100% and we all see eye to eye
on the thing.

Ralph lost his I. D. Card, wallet, and everything the last day
in port. It's on report and has to see the executive officer before
he can get a new one. Boy is he blue.

Darling, I'll be so glad when I can come back home to you and
we can float off on that cloud to paradise. What a beautiful life
we have in store for us. I thank God every night for blessing my
life with your presence and your love.

I love you so, honey, I love you for what you are—the most
beautiful and perfect lady ever created. I shall have to leave
now 'til tomorrow night. Pleasant dreams, honey, I can hardly
wait to see you.

Goodnight
All My Love,
Bill

---

* The "deck division" of a Navy ship consisted of boatswain's mates and had
a reputation for being the group of sailors who worked the most and slept the
least. Their work was primarily manual labor such as chipping rust and
painting (operationmilitarykids.org/navy-boatswains-mate-bm/

Approaching Gibraltar

Saturday, Jan. 19, 1952

Dearest Darling,

Well, another uneventful day is ended. We had to get up at 4:00 this morning and we had General Quarters from 5:30 A.M. to 10:00 A.M. That was a bad way to start things out. We met up with the Roosevelt* and Tarawa† today. We hit Gibraltar Monday and leave the 26th.

I bought an electric razor from Jack Heneger. He won it at a bingo game the other night. It's a small one and does an excellent job with no chance of cutting yourself. I bought it for $8.00.

The weather here has been nice and warm. Almost every day has been sunny. We have worked steady since leaving Norva.

I reviewed my first book I had completed in Shillinger so I'm ready to take on book II. Sy is trying to get us 2 to 3 dance jobs in every port we hit. If we do that's the only time I'll go on liberty anywhere. I don't like to be treated like an animal and wait in line and then have to come back to the ship with a boat full of drunks. So I shan't go ashore except in a very few places.

---

* Commissioned in April 1945, the USS *Roosevelt* was an aircraft carrier making voyages through the Mediterranean, typically alternating schedules with the USS *Midway*. (history.navy.mil/research/histories/ship-histories/danfs/f/franklin-d-roosevelt-cvb-42.html)

† The USS *Tarawa* was an aircraft carrier commissioned at the end of WWII and reactivated in 1950, to support the Korean War. (history.navy.mil/research/histories/ship-histories/danfs/t/tarawa-i.html)

*Bea, honey, I miss you so much. I just feel so lost without you.
It's difficult to write anything interesting because the same
thing happens every day. I miss your tender touch and gentle
caress.*

*I don't dare think about the possibility of being transferred. It
would be too much to think about. I sure would like it, though.*

*Most of the fellows are going to go on tours. I would like to but
I feel that the money is more important.*

*Bea, I'll be so glad to be back home with you again. You've
given me so much happiness and love. You're so sweet and
gentle. I'll just want to kiss you and kiss you. I really mean it
when I say my life didn't start 'till I met you.*

*My eyes are getting heavy, honey, so I'd better close for now.
I'll be longing for the day I can come back home and be with
my little wife.*

Good Night,
All My Love,
Bill

P.S. I love you so much.

Sunday, Jan. 20, 1952

Dearest Bea,

It's taps now and I am down in the Band Room alone with my thoughts and memories—memories of my other life with you. I miss you so much, honey, I just can't make heads or tails out of anything without you here to guide me along. You're like the spark of life that makes a man tick. You're my impetus, my inspiration—that which is my whole life.

I remember us talking one time about how I wanted to be prominent, etc. I want people to look at you and say there goes Mr. Holston's wife. I want as many people as possible to meet the one pure, holy, and lovely thing that God has ever conceived. You're my everything—my life, my happiness, and my religion. Darling, you are my Achilles heel—without you I would be in an eternal world of no reproach. Bea, I can only say that old, trite, and greatly misused expression, "I love you," not for any convenient, sexual, or live for the minute thing—but a love that is of a wonderful relationship of two lives so closely interwound that it would be extremely difficult for one to distinguish one from the other. You have shown me so much about life and the meaning of life and at the same time you've given me a challenge. I try to be worthy of your love and devotion. There has been so much pleasure in the few months that I have been home. The laughs, my tasty (?) jokes, (you must admit that I do wake up in an extremely pleasant disposition, my occasional breakfast making (a grapefruit isn't too difficult to fix, is it?).

I never dreamed that life could be so enjoyable and enlightening. I shall never forget our trips we made to Washington, Lynchburg, and Danville. It felt so great to have you by my side and feel like you're really accomplishing something. I hope I'll be able to start back soon. I just feel so lost and out of place here.

We're officially relieving the Roosevelt tomorrow. They're bringing their legendary court and eleven members of the band aboard here. We have to play for them and stand by all day for honors. What a drag that'll be.

Well, my sweet, it's time for me to go to sleep. Just 14 days ago I went to sleep with my arms around you—tonight—nothing.

Goodnight, darling. I love you so much. Be a sweet little girl and don't forget to eat your Wheaties in the morning. * Sweet Dreams.*

All My Love,
Bill

---

* This is suspected to be an inside joke based on their recent weeks together during the holidays.

Chapter 9

The World of Memories

At my grandparents' house the night of Bea's memorial service, everything felt off. Reuniting with my entire extended family *except Bea* was bewildering and disorienting.

Attempting to make something—anything—feel normal, my cousins, sister, and I wandered upstairs to the loft, where, during our teenage years, we would hang out and watch TV after big family dinners. I joined my cousins escaping to the mindlessness of a movie. My sister, Courtney, rummaged through boxes of family mementos and photographs.

After a while, she drew our attention away from the TV to a metal, fire-safe box, from which she pulled out a neat stack of letters. Each envelope was framed with an iconic red, white, and blue border and marked "via air mail."

Courtney removed the crinkly yellow pages from an envelope and began reading the correspondence. Her eyes suddenly widened.

"These are *definitely* love letters," she said, an eyebrow raised. "And I don't think we should read these now."

At that, my older sister wisely insinuated that we shouldn't read such personal correspondence while Shoopa was right downstairs. And I think we would all agree that, at the time, it felt weird to think of our grandparents as love-struck boyfriend and girlfriend.

She tucked the old mail away in a safe place so that after we went our separate ways, we'd know where to find the box of mail. Bea had saved it for a reason. We held out hope that the letters would bring a piece of her back to us again one day.

'Til death us do part

During the years that followed Bea's death, the unspeakable pain of her disappearance from our lives was intensified by witnessing Shoopa attempt mundane, everyday life without her. For my entire life, Bea-and-Shoopa had rolled off the tongue as if it were one word. And now it *was* one word.

Shoopa. Just Shoopa.

We quickly discovered that 56 years of marriage had not prepared him to be *just Shoopa*.

For everyone in our family, the four years that followed were a season of intense grief. But no one spun as out of control as Shoopa. During their marriage, Bea had served as the anchor that kept him from lunging toward one impulsive idea after the next. Without Bea, Shoopa was adrift in a world without boundaries.

Two years later, our grief was compounded by the unexpected loss of Bea and Shoopa's youngest daughter, my Aunt Jill. My cousins, sister, and I returned to Pensacola for the memorial service. The house on Bayou Chico felt even emptier. The grandfather we knew and loved, who had created such a magical childhood for us, now stared back at us with frustrated, tired eyes. In an interaction I wish I could forget, he yelled and threw his keys against the hardwood floor. Two years of carrying on through profound grief had taken an unbelievable toll.

Shoopa continued teaching at the Pensacola School of

Liberal Arts into his 80s. Shortly before his 81st birthday, he was hospitalized. I flew from our duty station in Guam to Florida for a final visit and was met with the grandfather I knew and loved. His brow had softened. His eyes once again held a sparkle. He seemed much calmer. Not long after, in May 2011, he passed away due to complications from prostate cancer, which he had lived with since the initial diagnosis some 20 years before.

In Shoopa's final earthly hours, at the house on Bayou Chico, my mom played the PHS Band's rendition of "Stars and Stripes Forever," as Shoopa spoke his last words.

"Bea is here. She is present. And it is *bea-utiful*."

With those words, the man who had spent his life teaching shared one more lesson with us. His longing for Bea never wavered, even into his final breaths.

The week after Shoopa passed away, our family returned to Pensacola alongside his former students, band members, sailing buddies, and longtime Navy friends. The stories of Bea and Shoopa's impact on so many lives were freshly told and were a tremendous source of comfort.

A short while later, my mom reminded me about the box of letters Courtney found, but my husband and I were living across the Pacific Ocean in Guam. Given the extreme distance and unreliable mail service to the island, I didn't want to risk the letters getting lost. So, I waited.

The following year, we moved duty stations to the East Coast. A short while later, our daughter, Sadie, was born. Nick deployed, and I navigated an exhausting new season of solo parenting. In the busyness of life as a new mom, I forgot about the letters.

More than life itself

Something about the tiny face of our daughter, the gift of new life, a fresh limb on the family tree, witnessing my own mother transform into a grandmother, and seeing our daughter form a special bond with her grandparents—these new milestones made me ache for more time with my grandparents.

I longed for the glory days at Bea and Shoopa's house on Bayou Chico, the endless summer afternoons fishing with cousins, skipping from boat to boat along the rugged wooden dock. I ached for Bea's handwriting in my mailbox, for her phone call on my birthday, for a chance to spend one more grand family dinner listening to big band tunes around their dining table then escaping to watch movies in the loft with my cousins.

Even more, I longed for Sadie, and later our son, Nate, to meet this inspirational couple who made such a tremendous impact on me and so many others. I imagined what it would be like for Bea to hold a great-grandchild in her arms. I mourned with fresh tears the loss of knowing this dream could never come true.

Shortly after Nick returned from his overseas tour and we celebrated Sadie's first birthday, my mom offered to bring the letters to Virginia. Without shipping risks to contend with and on the other side of our first deployment as parents, the timing finally seemed right to peek inside the envelopes.

On a summer day three years after Shoopa passed away, I opened one of the letters, unfolding the crinkly pages. I read my grandfather's faded handwriting. For the first time in three years, I heard his voice again—my heart leaping with every word.

The most marvelous letters

The contents of the box proved remarkable. Reading the postmark dates, I discovered that the stack of letters was written during my grandparents' first year of marriage. I knew that Bea and Shoopa were married on April 7, 1951. The first letter picked up seven short weeks later as the USS *Midway* left Naval Operating Base Norfolk through the Chesapeake Bay and journeyed south in the Atlantic toward Cuba.

With each letter I carefully unfolded and read, this unique season of my grandparents' journeys pressed further into my heart. For the first time in my life, I found myself face-to-face with my grandmother and grandfather as madly-in-love newlyweds. I was transported, somewhat magically, to a Bea and Shoopa, who had their whole lives ahead of them.

Sentence after scribbly sentence, the cadence of Shoopa's words to Bea was so familiar. I could hear the exuberance of his voice again. And yet, with each letter I unfolded, I found myself discovering him—discovering them—in a way I had never known before.

Everything inside the letters captivated me. But what stood out most was how the personality traits and values Bill illustrated in his writings in 1951, were remarkably synonymous with the Bea and Shoopa my cousins, sister, and I came to know and love half a century later. The mischief and fanfare, Shoopa's love of music and literature, Bea's dedication to work and family—all of it was captured in these pages.

Another stunning discovery was that the envelopes were addressed to Bea at Simpson's Trailer Park in Norfolk, Virginia. A search in *The Virginian-Pilot* archives revealed the park's location at a prominent intersection seven miles away.

As I opened each letter, I tried to imagine Bea's excitement walking to her mailbox, discovering the mail, unfolding this *exact piece of paper* from this same envelope, just seven miles from where I sat reading the same words six decades later.

Hearing Shoopa's voice on every page made me instantly wish to share his words. One day during the stillness of Sadie's nap time, I began transcribing each letter onto my laptop. I enjoyed the process tremendously, especially how it forced me to slow down and ingest every word my grandfather had written aboard the heartless ship that had carried him away from his beloved bride.

When the last letter was transcribed, I printed the collection to share with family and close friends. My grandfather's words were instantly cherished. My cousin, Chris, and his wife, Stacey, chose to read the collection slowly, one letter at a time, so they could savor every sentence.

In a family group text, we all laughed about Shoopa's apparent obsession with the vacuum cleaner. As much as we enjoyed hearing our grandparents' voices again, it was equally enjoyable to learn so many new things from a season of their lives none of us had experienced.

Only one more letter from the USS *Midway* remains to share. And for the lovestruck couple, it's an exciting one.

Chapter 10

News — January 24, 1952

The last letter found from aboard the USS Midway was written from Gibraltar.

Thursday PM: Jan 24, 1952

My Dearest Bea,

> *Darling, at last my orders are here. We're going to the Brooklyn Naval Yard!! We shall be able to have a marvelous time while we're there. I seem to be having trouble getting transportation from 6th fleet. I want to go back on the Roosevelt but they're leaving tomorrow at 1:00. So if I don't make that, I'll probably have to wait until I get to Augusta. This red tape is sure aggravating. I can see the Roosevelt just a few hundred feet from us. The whole 6th fleet is here with about ½ of it going back. Well, one thing is definite, I shall leave as soon as possible.*

> *The boys seem to be genuinely sorry to see me leave. Joe is very*

downcast and claims I am his only salvation. Dan Santaviecia got Pensacola, Fla. He seems to be in favor of it.

Yesterday we went over to the F. D. R. with the basketball team to play a game. We took the square and dance band. We played dance band at the half and the people enjoyed it a lot. Their band, so one of the fellows who was at the school with me said, it is very sad. He said the chief doesn't care and they play acey ducy all day. They aren't good enough to play for the movies!!! We rehearsed all day on the tunes we were to play and the band sounded real great.

We had a difficult time boarding the Roosevelt. The water was throwing the liberty boat into the side of the F. D. R. We were thoroughly drenched by the spray and the salt dried on our blues, leaving a coat of white that's almost impossible to get off.

I am going to pack everything today and be ready to leave at a moments notice.

Well, darling, it'll be easy sailing from here on out. Don't expect me home 'til about the middle or latter part of February. I can't wait to see you.

All My Love,
Bill

P.S. I love you, honey. It's going to be so great to be home again.
P.S. Jr. Please get the overload springs trailer hitch and the car wired. Have Mr. French check everything.

(same letter) January 21

> BULLETIN: My orders just came to leave immediately on the
> Roosevelt. I have to leave in a few minutes. See you Feb. 1-4.
> All my love, darling, have the car fixed. God bless you. I have
> 10 days leave (they made a mistake, I have 29 to the good) +
> 4 days proceed time + 2 days travel time. All in all 16 days. I
> am too excited to think about anything except I love you
> intensely.

See ya in 15 days—
All My Love,
Bill

Chapter 11

In the years that follow

"*I have so many wonderful memories and to think that our life together has only started! We have everything to which to look forward!*"

William J. Holston, Nov. 8, 1951

In January 1952, when the USS *Midway* pulled away from Norfolk, Bea and Bill were likely bracing to spend the full five months apart. Though Bill was told his orders may come in, they both knew the uncertainty of the Korean War or Cold War could have called for additional ships and personnel at a moment's notice.

Thankfully for Bill and Bea, there were no major interruptions to the timeline, and this final separation lasted only about a month. In Gibraltar, Bill got orders to the Brooklyn Naval Yard. With Bea in his heart and home in his sights, he crossed the Atlantic again on the USS *Roosevelt*, the *Midway's* sister ship.

What's missing from this collection of letters is what I can attest is the best day of deployment. That day is homecoming.

In our 20-plus years of Navy separations, my husband has never returned home from deployment on a ship. But after experiencing eight of his homecomings from various overseas tours, I can daydream about what this reunion might have been like for my grandparents. The carrier pulling through the cold chop of the Chesapeake Bay toward the James River. The scramble to find each other among thousands of deboarding sailors. The magical moment they first locked eyes. The warmth and wonder of that first glorious reunion kiss.

Within days of Shoopa's homecoming, they packed up the trailer and said goodbye to his sister, Peggy, and their nephew and nieces in Norfolk. A postcard to Bill's parents in Lynchburg, postmarked Feb. 14, 1952, indicates the couple found a waterfront view site at Johnson's Trailer Camp in Bayonne, New Jersey.

Later that year, Bill was honorably discharged from the Navy. He went on to study music and English at New York University. Hints from family correspondence reveal this boat lover from rural Virginia did not enjoy the cold winters of the Northeast or the crowded subways of the big city. He eventually finished his music degree at Florida State University in Tallahassee.

In 1954, Bill began his first teaching job as a high school band director in a tiny town in southern Georgia. The day after the couple's fourth wedding anniversary, he and Bea welcomed their first daughter, Jane (my mother).

Soon after, the couple moved to Pensacola, Florida, having no idea that's where they would call home for the rest of their lives. Fresh out of the Navy, young, ambitious Bill accepted a job as the band director at Pensacola High School.

Though his total enlistment was relatively short, Bill's time in the Navy Band greatly impacted his leadership at PHS. Under his direction, theirs was the only high school marching band in the state of Florida to play in President John F. Kennedy's Inaugural Parade.

The PHS band won several awards for their superior patriotic medleys, which Bill personally arranged. The PHS Band alumni have remained a tight-knit group, holding regular reunions throughout the decades that followed and, more recently, staying connected online.

In the 1960s, Bill served as a principal of Wedgewood Middle School and Woodham High School. Amid the instability of teacher strikes across Florida, he became disillusioned with the public school system. He set off on his own path and created a new school, the Pensacola School of Liberal Arts, which all three of their daughters attended. Bill served as the principal and language arts teacher, while Bea ran the administrative side, enrolling students and running the front office. Eventually, their daughter, Wendy, joined Bea in the office, and their daughter, Jill, taught classes.

For more than 40 years, the couple owned and operated this unique private school, which met the educational needs of 7th through 12th grade students in the Pensacola and Gulf Breeze areas. Some alumni from the school have gone on to become celebrated musicians, actors, and professors. The school is still in operation today.

In a recent conversation with Charles Cetti, one of Bill's band students at Pensacola High School, I was reminded why my grandfather was so revered for his teaching.

"Other than my parents, Mr. Holston had more influence on my development as an adult than anyone else," Cetti said. "Yes, he was the band director, but that wasn't his primary accomplishment. He used music as a vehicle to instruct students on how to become successful adults. He taught students how to follow directions. He taught students how to work in cooperation with others. He taught all the essential components of being a good adult. Hundreds of other kids who went through the band would say the same thing."

As a granddaughter, I was never Bea and Shoopa's student in a classroom setting. But from watching and listening, I picked up lasting lessons from each of them about books and boats, family and friends, faith, and love.

It remains one of the greatest gifts imaginable that those lessons were able to continue thanks to a neat stack of letters tucked away to be discovered when the time was right. As it happened, by a grandchild—at the precise moment of goodbye.

Chapter 12

A Bea utiful Surprise

Shortly after Bea passed away, my husband's sweet mother wrote me a letter sharing how much, decades later, she still deeply missed her grandmother. I will never forget her kindness in not trying to cheer me up. Instead, she shared something as painful to hear as it was helpful—that losing a beloved grandparent is a unique kind of sorrow that may never fully heal.

Saying goodbye to Bea opened my eyes to see that there were all these people walking around, carrying on with life, quietly missing their grandparents. Blissfully sheltered for so many years, I had no idea such an awful club existed until I regretfully became part of it.

As the magnitude of Bea's absence grew, I poured out my heart in a letter to my sister, Courtney. "I know we are all struggling to cope with the new hole presented in our lives, a hole that's different for each of us. I'm realizing that for me, Bea was the person I would always call with good news or a fun story or an exciting experience. She was quick to listen and would be thrilled at whatever I had to say. I can still hear her voice saying, 'Well, Peyton, that's just wonderful!' And she always said it so genuinely, like it was the best story she'd ever heard."

To me, Bea's voice exuded pure love. Over time I found that hearing her voice was what I missed most of all.

Three years after saying goodbye to my grandfather, I devoured sentence after sentence of his *Midway* letters. His philosophical take on the military and his relationship with Bea transported me to their dinner table, to vibrant discussions during countless family meals. And I loved being able to witness him head over heels for Bea. His heartache for her stirred my own longings for this woman we both mutually adored.

After reading a stack of letters from Shoopa, I opened an envelope and discovered one not written by him. A single letter was written by Bea. It had been stashed away in a USS *Midway* bunk room, brought back to the mainland in Norfolk, towed in a trailer to New York, Georgia, and Florida, preserved in a fire-safe metal box to be discovered generations later.

The note from Bea that follows is one of the four letters Shoopa mentions in his letter dated November 8, 1951. The sweet poem she wrote is undated and reveals a few key details about their dating relationship.

Exciting as it was to read her responses to Shoopa, what gripped me most was Bea's honey voice falling fresh on my ears one more time. For a moment after reading it, I sat at my dining table, tears blurring my vision, a glow of pure love warming my soul.

For those of you who don't know my grandmother, Bea, I am so pleased to introduce the young woman with the starring role in each of the previous letters. If you haven't met her, her voice may not captivate you as it does me. But I hope that, perhaps, her sweet words of encouragement to Shoopa will stir in your heart your own memories of a voice that represents pure love.

Nov 5, 1951
Monday night

My Darling,

Never have I been as thrilled as I was today, when the mail revealed not one, but two letters from you. Today, at the office, I opened the Midway mail, and took in 132 requisitions from the mighty CVB 41. I tried to tell myself that I could hardly expect a letter so soon, but it was all I could do to contain myself until I got home! I have read both letters three times so far, and each time I'm thrilled to my toes. Darling—you write the most marvelous letters. I think you should be an author instead of a musician!

There is rumor around the office that I'll start working half a day on Saturday—alternating with the other girls. (Have I told you this before?). I really don't think I have been there long enough to be left alone, and besides, I just hate working on Saturday, even if it's only half a day, once a month.

Peggy said that Grace (or was it Helen?) Cavalier dropped in on her the other evening—with her husband! She had just arrived South, having gone on to Texas, when Harry's ship came into Norfolk—so up she drove! He's going to stay home long enough to build a house after this trip, before signing up for another one. What a life!?!

I received several things today—your two letters. (They head the list, of course), the allotment (which I am depositing tomorrow—to bring our savings account total to $330) and a savings Bond from the office. That makes two $25 bonds from the office and two that my grandfather gave me. We should get a deposit box at the bank.

Darling – you say such wonderful and sweet things. I just hope that I can live up to your expectations, always. I always want to be at your side—to help you, encourage you, and love you to pieces! And when circumstances are such that you have to be away, you know that I am waiting for you—in our own home —thinking of you and loving you every minute of the day and night.

Don't you think you aren't doing the Navy any good. You are giving it your time, your energies, your talents, and several years of your life. The Navy is extremely fortunate to have you in its midst. I think it should give you a little something in return – like a nice show station! Remember – "There's a job for you, in navy blue"!!!

You should see my curls – I have a headful. Tonight I'm going to bed without putting my hair up – and there is absolutely no one to witness this rare event.

My sweet – I am almost crazy with excitement – waiting for your arrival. I'm dying to see you, your suntan and the weight you have gained (?).

Your letter arrived in record time, as its post marked 12:00 P.M. Nov. 4th, and today is the 5th.

Goodnight, Bill. Hurry home—and we'll make up for all this lost time. I want to squeeze you and love you so much.

All my love,
Bea

The date of this poem by Bea is unknown. It references the time before their marriage when she was living and working in Washington, D.C.

> *It happened so suddenly, as you shall see,*
> *This wonderful change that came over me.*
> *It was a revelation that proved once again*
> *How God steers the lives of mortal men.*
>
> *My tale began one November night.*
> *I returned from work with no diversion in sight;*
> *My mailbox yielded nothing, so, covered with gloom,*
> *I pampered my emotions and sulked in my room.*
>
> *When the telephone rang, I jumped with glee,*
> *But I soon calmed down, for who would call me??*
> *Suddenly, I was stunned – had I bumped into a wall?*
> *No – "Long distance for 322" resounded through the*
> *   hall!!*
>
> *Another shock followed when Bill's voice I heard.*
> *(I was so happy I almost purred)*
> *He's a handsome and talented sailor boy,*
> *And a southern gentleman from his head to his toe!*
>
> *He had been given a leave of fourteen days,*
> *And his following words were like sunshine rays:*
> *"Could you come to Lynchburg this weekend to see*
> *My home and family, and, of course, me!?"*
>
> *The evening that earlier so lonesome had been*
> *Was magically transformed into laughter and din.*
> *Although many months had passed since I last saw*
> *   Bill,*
> *The thoughts of his dimples still gave me a thrill!*

November 24th was the fateful day [*]
When I left D.C. and traveled Virginia way.
The long-planned day had come at last
And it will forever be a vivid part of my past.

---

[*] The fateful day refers to November 24, 1950, six months before they married. The long-distance call most likely came from Norfolk after the *Midway* returned from a four-month tour through the Mediterranean.

Chapter 13

Shoopa's Final Letter

The following letter—the last found from Bill to Bea—was in an unmarked envelope containing no date or postmark. The letter is presumed to have been written during the summer of 1966, 15 years into the couple's marriage.

During his tenure as the Pensacola High School band director, Bill took a summer session at Florida State University (FSU) working on a Master of Public Administration. This summer session was the only other long period of separation the couple experienced during the rest of their 56-year marriage.

∽

Dear Bea,

> *The letter I just got was undoubtedly the finest literary effort I have ever seen. I have read Emerson, Jefferson, Thoreau, Marx, Franklin, etc., but never anything to begin to compare with my feelings to that masterpiece! This will go down as our greatest fulfillment. It is difficult to imagine a more meaningful marriage or bond of love and understanding than we have in*

our family. It is a wonderful experience to have such a family unit with three lovely children. We need to recognize these blessings for the future will hold tragedy, but with our particular sustaining faith, we shall weather any storm.

The odd thing about your being needed is a real understatement. The continuous dialogue from your husband, the only music opinion as to value for programs, etiquette rulings, clothes to wear, vocational goals in life, discipline problems ad infinitum were asked you because your opinion is the only opinion I have ever trusted more so than my own… for I don't have your depth of understanding nor your wisdom… but I am working in your direction. Maybe some day I'll approach a small part of what you already know.

On that day I shall arrive at the plateau that will transcend any known feeling or insight that has transpired since those frustrated days of the smooth-skinned 20 year-old has been attributed to the loving hand of you … in fact my mother would be the first to admit it!!!!!!

The boating idea is fantastic. We could derive a never known dimension with the serenity and closeness of nature. Somehow God and nature in the stillness of both… reinforces some inner nerve ends and refreshes like nothing of known value. With you and me experiencing this phenomenon together… well that is really too much to even contemplate.*

---

* Knowing Shoopa's eventual obsession with collecting boats, our family got a good laugh at the thought that the initial suggestion to own one might have come from Bea. The running joke was that any time Bea went out of town, Shoopa bought another boat. When Shoopa passed away in 2011, their dock on Bayou Chico was home to two large sailboats, the Viking Ship, a houseboat, and half a dozen small dinghies and sailboats, all in various states of disrepair. My sister, cousins, and I look back fondly on the countless boat stories and fishing memories from our time together on Bayou Chico.

I am eagerly awaiting Friday. I expect to be completely rested so that I can say I love you 5 million times. Life is so short at its longest… we will turn the shortness into love filled minutes so all the moments together will seem like ten lifetimes!

John Spratt* left me a note saying he has been suffering from the gout. I am going by to see him. He indicated he had hoped to go to Pensacola this weekend but cannot do so now.

Well my love to you… and to the children… See you Friday… Be prepared!

Lovingly,
Bill

Bill and Bea Holston with their daughters, (left to right) Jill, Jane and Wendy.

---

* John Spratt was a music professor at FSU who Bill had become close with during his undergraduate studies.

*Goodbye, my darling. I love you, a love that grows stronger every day.
A love that will grow beyond the twilight of this life."*

William J. Holston, USS Midway, May 31, 1951

Chapter 14

Epilogue: My Letter to You

Dear Reader,

From the moment I opened the first envelope 10 years ago, these letters became an instant treasure, allowing me to hear my grandparents' voices again. The more I read and studied these pages, the more treasures they revealed. As this story comes to an end, a letter feels like the perfect way to share a few final revelations with you.

A truly priceless gift is that the letters introduced me to my grandmother as a newly married Navy spouse—the same role I found myself in while reading these pages 60 years later. This realization first sparked as I sat at the dining table of our rental house in Virginia Beach reading the words Shoopa sent to Bea at a trailer park in the next town over. Her husband was away. My husband was away. Generations apart, Bea and I kept ourselves busy tending to work and family as we awaited our loved one's return.

The more I considered how our circumstances over-lapped, the more questions emerged that I wish I had asked Bea. Questions like, what was it like to marry someone in the Navy while the Korean War was underway? What were their favorite local places? Did they walk the same sandy shores we did? Did they catch fish and swim in the same salty waters where their great-grandchildren now do?

I will likely never know the answers. But I appreciate how the letters helped me discover the questions.

Something else I noticed from reading their correspondence so many times was that Bea and I shared a common struggle as a military spouse—having a career. Bea never stated this outright. But letter after letter, Shoopa's empathetic replies tell of her limited job options, dissatisfaction with her employer, and lamenting having to work when her sailor was home and on leave.

Decades later, despite all that has changed in military life (and life in general), I've experienced similar frustrations trying to hold down a job and plan around my husband's sporadic schedule. (I have no doubt this frustration resonates with others who are tied to someone with unconventional work hours).

These letters show me that Bea would have understood many of the work-related struggles I've faced. Because, as a Navy spouse, she faced them too.

Another revelation from the letters shines light on the four difficult years after Bea passed away. Discovering on every page the depth of young Bill's love for Bea, I saw with new eyes the deep grief our family watched him wade through when she suddenly left our lives.

My grandfather's love for Bea was so intense that once she died, he became untethered. Letter after homesick letter make it clear that Shoopa's heart was only at peace when together with Bea.

From his bunk room on the Midway, Shoopa wrote, "… since you came into my life it doesn't make sense without you" (June 4, 1951). He said, "… without you life wouldn't mean a <u>thing</u>" (Nov. 5, 1951). He wrote, "I just can't make heads or tails out of anything without you here to guide me along" (Jan. 20, 1952).

When Shoopa wrote these letters as a 21-year-old newly-wed, the separation had been bearable because it was temporary. He knew they'd be reunited when the ship returned home to Norfolk. But when Bea passed away after 56 years of marriage, the hope of being together no longer existed in the same way.

This may explain why after Bea's death, Shoopa commissioned a life-sized mural of the resurrected Jesus Christ, arms wide open, floating on clouds, to be painted on the dining room wall across from his easy chair. Perhaps he needed visible hope of seeing Bea again in order to make it through every hour without her.

One last bit of treasure I feel compelled to share is that the main reason these letters exist is because of the geographic separation brought on by my grandfather's naval service. We've all heard it said that absence makes the heart grow fonder. Had my grandparents settled in together after their wedding and worked local jobs, there wouldn't have been such a compelling reason for Shoopa to put his young love in writing week after week.

This insight may sound obvious, but it has helped me strangely appreciate the most difficult aspect of my post-9/11 military relationship—the long and lonely months living apart from the man I chose to spend my life with. At our first married duty station in Coronado, California, as simultaneous wars in Iraq and Afghanistan dragged on, I spent more months by myself than I did with Nick—not unlike Bea's first year of marriage to Shoopa.

On countless walks around the island, I recall gazing across San Diego Bay where the USS *Midway* now rests, decommissioned and operating as a museum. I knew my grandfather had served aboard the mighty vessel. When I attended work events on the *Midway's* flight deck, I imagined Shoopa spending untold months of his young adult life sleeping in one of the many bunks below. But that's the extent of what I knew about his time on board as a sailor.

Now, with these letters in hand, I can see it is the Navy that was responsible for creating the separation that led my grandfather to pour out his lovesick heart. Strangely, I owe a debt of gratitude to "this tub," the USS *Midway*, for carrying Shoopa away from his dearest Bea so we could witness their sweet young love decades later.

My husband and I are soon approaching the end of his naval career, and the lessons from these letters make me wonder what unexpected gifts he and I will one day look back on from his years of military service. Perhaps the love letters from Plebe Summer, emails exchanged between home and warzones, heartfelt anniversary cards, riveting deployment stories, and incomparable friendships will eventually outshine the heartaches and sacrifices of 20 years of war.

Years after my grandparents left our lives, their letters stir this hope in my heart. I see so clearly now the infinite power love has when it is written down.

And therein, perhaps, lies an everlasting lesson for us all.

~

Dear Reader, thank you for joining me on this journey. It has been an incredible joy to celebrate my grandparents' love for one another and the mighty ship that served as a backdrop during their first year of marriage.

My hope is that the love in these letters finds its way into your heart and is shared with those around you—perhaps even as words on a page, slipped into in an envelope, to be saved and cherished for generations to come.

With love always,
Peyton

P.S. My favorite part of any letter is when someone writes back. I would *love* to hear from you! Please write to me any time:

- peyton-roberts.com/contact
- peytonrobertsauthor@gmail.com

I look forward to staying connected through the stories we share.

Appendix I
What to do with a stack of old letters

Whenever my grandfather's letters come up in conversation, I've heard others mention they, too, have a stack of old letters. Sometimes the conversation reveals a dilemma of how to handle such personal correspondence that was written by a loved one but addressed to someone else.

While, clearly, I've made a decision not only to read, but also to share, my grandfather's letters, this dilemma still resonates. When my sister found these letters the day of my grandmother's memorial service, our family had barely said goodbye to her. My sister, cousins, and I all agreed it didn't feel right to read the letters while my grandfather was right downstairs. In fact, it was several years after he passed away before the time felt right to peek inside the envelopes.

Others I've spoken to don't believe they will ever feel comfortable reading their parents' letters, but they can't bring themselves to toss them out, either. And so, the letters sit in a box in the attic, and a door to family history remains locked.

While working to preserve this collection, I have become aware of other options of what can be done besides transcribing the letters or throwing them out. And so, I have compiled a list of possibilities to consider for anyone who becomes the recipient of a stack of old letters.

- **Showcase the letters.** Whether or not you've read the letters, they can be turned into art by framing them, arranging the envelopes in a shadowbox, or placing them in a decorative container in a prominent place in your home.
- **Archive the letters.** If the letters are from a particular military unit, theater, or branch, a corresponding historical organization might be interested in archiving their contents. Search first for a military association related to the unit, conflict, or time period. If there isn't a designated association, search for a military museum, then a veteran's group. Those organizations should have a process for receiving original documents (typically scanned and emailed). If you no longer want the physical letters, the organization may accept originals.
- **Pass the letters along.** If reading a close family member's letters feels like an invasion of privacy, consider passing the correspondence down to grandchildren or more distanced friends or family members who would be interested in reading the contents. Ask that individual to relay any quotes or stories you might appreciate but spare you any overly intimate details.
- **Read the letters.** This is, of course, a very personal choice that depends on the nature of the letters and your relationship to the writer. Not everyone will feel comfortable reading the letters that were left behind—and that's okay.
- If you decide to read the letters, there are several ways to approach this. Before you begin, take some

time to place the letters in order by postmark. The letters will tell a more cohesive story read chronologically.

- If you have many letters (I once spoke to someone whose stack numbered in the hundreds), perhaps read a few at a time. Take notes and record your favorite lines into one document, noting the postmark date for reference.

- **Have the letters translated.** If the letters you have are written in a language you don't know, you might be able to find volunteers who will translate them. Reach out to museums and historical organizations associated with the country or conflict. The foreign language department at a local college may also be able to help with translation.

- **Transcribe the letters.** My decision to transcribe my grandfather's letters was twofold. First, I knew our family would join me in wanting to read his words to Bea. But we were spread across the country, and mailing the original collection felt risky. Transcribing the letters meant preserving my grandfather's words digitally and made the letters easy to share.

- An unexpected gift of transcribing the letters was that I sat with every word, spent a quiet moment with every sentence my grandfather and grandmother wrote. Their thoughts and feelings during this season of life became familiar to me. Missing them as much as I did, I enjoyed that feeling of closeness tremendously.

- **Print the letters as a book.** It's easier than ever to turn a Word document into a book using a user-friendly publishing platform like Blurb or Lulu. Others have simply printed the pages at an office

supply store or photocopied the pages and put
them in order in three-ring binder.

Turning the love letters into a book makes an inexpensive yet priceless gift for family and friends and preserves the words of the letter writer for future generations. And having a hard copy that sits on a coffee table or bookshelf is more accessible than a digital copy for referencing favorite stories and quotes.

As handwritten correspondence becomes a lost pastime, I believe old letters will become even more cherished. The sentiments and stories inside unlock a door to the past, allowing loved ones to live on vibrantly in our hearts long after goodbye.

Whether or not you choose one of these options above, I hope you will consider taking steps to preserve the words in your care. Letters have a way of transcending time and bringing love back to life. In that regard, they may be the closest we can get to experiencing pure magic.

Appendix II

Obituaries & Eulogy

Beatrice Estelle McGlasson Holston
1930-2007

Beatrice "Bea" McGlasson Holston, age 76, passed away

peacefully, on May 29, 2007, at her home in Pensacola, surrounded by her family.

Bea was born in 1930, in Lausanne, Switzerland, to Boija Pospisilova and Clifford McGlasson, who was Vice Consul for the United States Foreign Service. Bea lived in various locations throughout Europe, arriving in Washington, D.C., in 1941, where she met her soulmate, Bill Holston.

Bill and Bea relocated to Pensacola in 1955, where she joined First United Methodist Church. She particularly enjoyed nature, music, travel, and caring for others. Bill and Bea founded the Pensacola School of Liberal Arts in 1969, which aimed to provide personalized quality education to young people in Northwest Florida.

Bea's proudest accomplishments were being an exceptional wife, mother, and grandmother. She is survived by her loving husband of 56 years, William J. Holston; daughters Jane, Wendy and Jill; grandchildren: Courtney, Peyton, Chris, and Erika; and many extended family members and friends.

William Joseph Holston
1930-2011

William Joseph "Bill" Holston of Pensacola passed away peacefully on Tuesday, May 10, 2011, surrounded by the love of his faith family.

Born in Lynchburg, Virginia, young "Billy Joe" had an adventurous childhood on the James River where he discovered his lifelong passion for music and mischief. He attended Lynchburg College where he excelled in music and sports. He then joined the U. S. Navy where he traveled the world playing trumpet in an elite USN band onboard the USS *Midway*.

Bill met the love of his life, Beatrice McGlasson, while living in Washington, D.C., and they married and relocated to New York, where he continued his music education at NYU. A perpetual student, Bill earned a master's from Florida State University, and in 1955, was recruited as Band Director for Pensacola High School.

The Holstons moved to Pensacola where Bill taught band

and humanities for 12 years and raised their three daughters. Bill was a composer, musician, and teacher; and, under his inspired direction, the PHS Fighting Tiger Band was the only high school from the State of Florida invited to march at the inauguration of President John F. Kennedy.

Bill earned a master's in public administration in 1967, after which he was chosen as principal of Wedgewood Middle and Woodham High Schools in Escambia County. 'Mr. Holston,' as he is called by his students, was known for his sparkling wit and interactive teaching style, replete with lessons from history and literature. Love of the sea and seafaring adventures became a trademark theme throughout his career.

In 1969, Bill and Bea Holston embarked on a unique educational voyage, as they founded and nurtured the Pensacola School of Liberal Arts, a private school which enabled thousands of young people to develop their individual and intellectual potential in a personal atmosphere. Together, Bill and Bea were educational advocates, humanitarians, and leaders who helped young people and their parents to aspire, achieve, and advance.

Bill's proudest accomplishment was his family. He was an exceptional husband, father, and "Shoopa" to his grandchildren. He lived an extraordinary life focused on inspiring the young and old alike to reach for their wildest hopes and dreams while keeping their feet firmly planted. He was a faithful servant of God and valued counselor and mentor to his friends, neighbors, students, and their families. He will forever be remembered as a teacher, visionary, philosopher, and a great man who truly made a difference in the world.

William Holston was preceded in death by his beloved wife of 56 years, Beatrice Holston, his daughter and professional colleague, Dr. Jill Holston; his parents, Joseph and Irene Holston; and his sister, Margaret "Peggy" Tashner Holston.

He is survived by his loving daughters, Jane Holston and Wendy Anderson; four grandchildren, Courtney Holston-Toth, Peyton Roberts, Christopher Thomas, and Erika Thomas; many nieces, nephews, and cousins; and a host of students, colleagues, and friends who cherish his memory.

Remarks spoken at Bill Holston's memorial service can be found at peyton-roberts.com/mydearestbea.

The Viking Ship

In the 1970s and 80s, the Viking Ship, named the *Loki*, operated as a floating museum. In 1977, Bill Holston led a crew of students and teachers on a 1,300 mile voyage across the Gulf of Mexico to Cozumel. In 2004, the ship was badly damaged during Hurricane Ivan. Now it rests on shore in front of Joe Patti's Seafood, a beloved seafood market in historic Pensacola.

About the Editor

Shoopa's 81st birthday and my last visit with him.

Peyton H. Roberts is a writer whose stories have appeared in *The New York Times*, Modern Love Podcast, Military.com, and more. Her novel *Beneath the Seams* (Scrivenings Press) explores the human cost of clothing. Inspired by true events in the global fashion industry, the story was selected as a book club pick by *Military Families Magazine*.

Peyton grew up in Pensacola, Florida, where she enjoyed sailing, fishing, sewing, and publishing books in her very best cursive. Her own Navy romance began in 2001 shortly before the 9/11 attacks, which ushered in two decades of long-distance separations and wartime deployments.

Peyton currently lives in Virginia Beach with her husband and two boat-loving children, Sadie and Nate. They enjoy sunny days on the water and catching their dinner together.

Keep in touch with Peyton at peyton-roberts.com.

Made in United States
Orlando, FL
12 June 2025

62005263R10080